Y0-CJI-310

ENNIS AND NANCY HAM LIBRARY
ROCHESTER COLLEGE
800 WEST AVON ROAD
ROCHESTER HILLS, MI 4830

LIVERWORTS
OF
SOUTHERN MICHIGAN

WILLIAM CAMPBELL STEERE

CRANBROOK INSTITUTE OF SCIENCE

LIVERWORTS
OF
SOUTHERN MICHIGAN

WILLIAM CAMPBELL STEERE

CRANBROOK INSTITUTE OF SCIENCE
BULLETIN NO. 17 JANUARY, 1940

COPYRIGHT 1940

BY THE CRANBROOK INSTITUTE OF SCIENCE

BLOOMFIELD HILLS, MICHIGAN

Lithoprinted by CUSHING-MALLOY, Inc., 1950 from the original
printing by the Cranbrook Press

Contents

Preface 4

Frontispiece 6

Introduction 7

The structure and reproduction of liverworts 9

Where liverworts grow 12

How to collect and keep liverworts 13

How to identify liverworts 15

A key to the genera of liverworts of southern Michigan . . 17

The liverworts of southern Michigan 22

Glossary 94

Index to the genera and species 96

Preface

Liverworts of Southern Michigan is a relatively non-technical handbook designed for those who wish to learn to identify and to recognize at sight the commoner members of an interesting but often overlooked group of plants. The author will be glad to extend personal aid to beginners and invites them to submit their more puzzling specimens to him for naming.

Frontispiece
RICCIOCARPUS NATANS ×3.

Photograph by the author

Liverworts of Southern Michigan

By WILLIAM CAMPBELL STEERE

University of Michigan

Introduction

LIVERWORTS are diminutive plants which, with the true mosses, compose the division Bryophyta of the Plant Kingdom. They are too small for casual identification with the naked eye by persons unfamiliar with them. Consequently, in spite of their beautiful symmetry and delicate structure, liverworts have been neglected by both amateur and professional botanists, as their almost complete lack of common names will attest. With a reasonably good hand-lens, however, anyone interested in plants may learn to know the Michigan liverworts.

The purpose of this small volume is to make possible the recognition and identification of Michigan liverworts in the field or in the laboratory, without the necessity of using a microscope. The non-technical descriptions, supplemented by photographs and drawings, are designed for beginners, not for professional bryologists.

Every plant has many common names. Those familiar to people in one region are often unknown in another. Furthermore, the same common name is often used for different plants in various parts of the country. This creates confusion. To avoid it, botanists have given each plant a scientific name, by which it is known internationally. Regardless of one's geographical location or the language he speaks, the specific plant indicated by a scientific name is clear. For this reason, only scientific names are given for the liverworts described here.

In every field of knowledge there are certain words which are more aptly descriptive than others. Often these are unfamiliar to persons not acquainted with that particular subject. Their use, however, is essential to accurate description. Because liverworts differ in many respects from other plants, a special vocabulary is needed to describe them. These unusual terms are all defined in the glossary.

Liverworts, like most plants, are at present of no particular economic importance to man. Consequently, it is interesting and often amusing to read in the early botanical works known as herbals the quaintly worded accounts of the surprising virtues of liverworts. Nearly four centuries ago the following passage concerning "Stone Liverwort" (our present day *Marchantia polymorpha*) appeared in Dodoens' "A Niewe Herball" (1578):

> "Stone Liverwort spreadeth itselfe abroade upon the ground, having wrinckled, or crimpled leaves layde one upon another as the scales of fishe, and are greene on the upper part, and browne on that side which is next the ground: amongst the leaves there grow up smal stemmes or twigges, in the toppes whereof are certayne knappes or things like starres. The rootes are like smal threddes, growing under the leaves, whereby it cleaveth, and sticketh fast upon the ground, and upon moyst or sweating rockes. This herbe (if a man may so cal it) groweth in moyst groundes, and stonie places, and shadowie, where as the Sonne shineth seldome. It bringeth foorth his starres in June and July. Liverwort is colde and drie of complexion. The decoction of Liverworte, swageth the inflammation of the liver, & openeth the stoppinges of the same, and is very good agaynst fever tertians, and all inflammations of blood. This herbe (as Dioscorides and Plinie writeth) brused when it is yet greene, and layd upon woundes, stoppeth the superfluous bleeding of the same and preserveth them both from inflammation and Apostemation. The same doth also heale all foule scurffes and spreading scabbes, as the Pockes, and wildefire, and taketh away the markes and scarres made with hoate irons, if it be pounde with hony and layde thereupon. The same boyled in wine, and holden in the mouth, stoppeth the Catarrhes, that is, a distilling or falling downe of Reume, or water and flegme from the brayne to the throte."

Although liverworts are occasionally used as aquarium and terrarium plants by botanists, their real suitability for these purposes remains practically unknown to amateurs. The fundamental importance of liverworts lies, of course, in their ability to absorb and retain relatively large amounts of water. They, as well as mosses, prevent rapid run-off of rain and so help to check erosion. Since they act as reservoirs of moisture, liverworts (and mosses) are important in the biological balance of nature as breeding places for insects and other small animals, as well as excellent propagation beds for plant seeds, especially those of trees.

The Structure and Reproduction of Liverworts

THE NAME "liverwort" was originally applied to plants without a leafy stem consisting only of a flat, ribbon-like or heart-shaped body of green tissue, called a *thallus*. This original concept of liverworts has been extended to include the "Scale Mosses," plants with leafy stems, because of their obviously close relationship, so that we must now distinguish between thallose and leafy liverworts.

All liverworts grow and reproduce in a fundamentally similar manner. The green plant *(gametophyte)*, whether thallose or leafy, possesses the pigment chlorophyll, and so can make its own food. Most liverworts are also provided with root-hair-like *rhizoids,* by means of which they obtain water and mineral salts, and are anchored to their substratum. Many plants produce small bud-like outgrowths, called *gemmae,* composed of from few to many cells, according to the species, each of which is able to produce a new green plant. Although some liverworts reproduce rapidly by their gemmae, the usual means of reproduction is very different. At some time during the year most liverworts produce minute, flask-shaped structures, the *archegonia,* each archegonium containing one egg in the swollen basal part; and small, spherical to elliptical, stalked structures, the *antheridia,* each antheridium producing many free-swimming *sperms* or *antherozoids*. When the plants are wet with dew or rain, the antherozoids swim through the thin film of water to the archegonium, down its neck, and one of them unites with the egg. *Fertilization,* which is the union of the sperm with the egg, does not lead directly to the formation of a new green plant. On the contrary, the fertilized egg, still within the archegonium, divides into a mass of cells which eventually become a spherical to short-cylindric case filled with *spores*. The spore-case or *capsule* may be one or more layers of cells thick, and in most liverworts is on the upper end of a white stalk or *seta* varying in length from 1 to 50 mm. At the base of the stalk is a swollen absorbing organ, the *foot,* through which the capsule receives most of its food and water. The capsule generally remains within the greatly swollen archegonium (now called the *calyptra*) until mature, when it bursts out as the result of the sudden and rapid growth of the stalk. The contents of the capsule do not become transformed entirely into spores, but also into minute thread-like *elaters* curiously ornamented with internal spiral bands, which aid in the dissemination of the spores. After their escape from the capsule, the spores germinate and produce new green plants, thus completing the life cycle. The green plant, because it produces the sperm and egg, or *gametes,* is called the *gametophyte,* whereas the capsule, together with the seta and foot makes up the spore-producing part of the plant, or *sporophyte,* which is almost completely dependent or parasitic upon the green gametophyte.

The variability of both gametophyte and sporophyte enables us not only to arrange the liverworts in an orderly manner, but to identify them reasonably easily. The most generally accepted classification of the liverworts or hepatics (class Hepaticae) is as follows:

I. Order **Marchantiales:** Plant always a flat, ribbon-like or heart-shaped thallus, normally branching by a regular forking. Thallus showing, in cross section, a sharp differentiation into a solid, colorless, lower tissue and a green upper tissue filled with air chambers which communicate to the oustide by means of more or less clearly defined epidermal pores. In some species the pores are *simple*, surrounded by a single layer of cells; in others they are *compound*, surrounded by a barrel-shaped ring of cells several layers thick. Capsule opening in various ways, but never by 4 regular valves.

1. Family RICCIACEAE: Thallus rarely more than 2.5 cm. long; archegonia and antheridia scattered, rarely in distinct groups; sporophyte consisting of capsule only, foot and stalk lacking; elaters absent.

2. Family MARCHANTIACEAE: Thallus sometimes reaching 15 cm. in length; antheridia and archegonia distinctly in groups, and in many species, on stalked receptacles; sporophyte consisting of capsule, stalk, and foot; elaters present.

II. Order **Jungermanniales:** Plant body either a thallus or a leafy stem, its tissues slightly or not at all differentiated, with neither air chambers nor pores. Sporophyte always consisting of capsule, stalk, and foot, the stalk becoming much elongated at maturity, the capsule almost invariably opening by 4 valves; elaters present.

1. Family JUNGERMANNIALES ANACROGYNAE: Plant body a thallus or a thallus-like stem with rudimentary leaves.

2. Family JUNGERMANNIALES ACROGYNAE (Scale Mosses): Plant body leafy, distinctly flattened, the leaves normally arranged in three rows, two rows on the upper side of the stem, and one row on the lower side; the underleaves commonly much smaller than the upper, often being greatly reduced and not uncommonly entirely absent; leaves lacking a midrib and varied in shape, being either wholly undivided or variously fringed, toothed, lobed or deeply divided. In many species, a smaller lobe (lobule) is rolled or folded in under the larger upper one. The sporophyte is inconspicuous, its stalk not becoming elongated until maturity of the capsule and drying up almost immediately thereafter. The sporophyte is protected during development not only by the greatly enlarged archegonium or *calyptra,* but also by a tubular organ unique to this group, the *perianth*. The perianth consists of a hollow tube which is attached at the base and open at the tip. It is shaped variously according to the species, and in the majority of leafy liverworts it develops whether fertilization takes place or not.

III. Order **Anthocerotales** (Hornworts) : Only one family:

    1. Family ANTHOCEROTACEAE: Plant body a circular thallus with very little differentiation of cells, each cell usually containing a single large chloroplast. Sporophyte a green, horn-like structure, with stomata and air chambers, growing continually in length from just above the large foot which remains imbedded in the gametophyte, splitting into two valves above; elaters present, although ordinarily inconspicuous.

Where Liverworts Grow

THE MAJORITY of Michigan liverworts grow in places which are usually moist and shady. In the wooded areas of southern Michigan, liverworts will be found on rotten logs, on the base and trunk of trees, on shaded boulders, on hummocks of earth and humus, and on the steep banks of shaded ravines. In most spruce, tamarack and cedar bogs, liverworts are common and form a conspicuous part of the vegetation. In the open, floating bogs which surround small, stagnant lakes, many characteristic species of liverworts grow among the hummocks of peat moss *(Sphagnum)*. Although the greater number of Michigan liverworts prefer constantly moist places, some are able to withstand extreme habitats. For example, a few grow actually in standing or flowing water, whereas others grow characteristically on the trunk of trees well above the ground, on exposed rocks, or in open, sandy fields, where their water supply is intermittent and casual. Although exposures of bedrock and the habitats they afford are rare in southern Michigan, they nevertheless support very characteristic species of liverworts, as will be seen from an examination of the cliffs at Grand Ledge and at the tip of Michigan's "thumb" in Huron County. A careful search of quarries and scattered bits of exposed bedrock will repay the seeker after new localities for rare species and may result in the discovery of species previously unknown in Michigan.

How to Collect and Keep Liverworts

IT IS DIFFICULT to give exact instructions about what to collect, as the beginner will know very few or no liverworts, and is even very apt to confuse them with lichens or mosses. Lichens, when green, have a dull grayish or bluish tinge very different from the clear to silvery green color of thallose liverworts. Furthermore, the characteristic cup-shaped fruiting bodies usually distinguish lichens. Mosses resemble leafy liverworts in their color, but are generally larger, and usually have more than three rows of leaves, which are not at all different on the lower side of the stem. Moss leaves are never fringed or lobed, but may have a prominent midrib, and more rarely a border of longer, narrower cells. The moss capsule does not split to the base in four regular valves, and is much larger and more solid than the liverwort capsule. Its stalk is stiff and, with the capsule, lasts from several months to several years, in great contrast to the ephemeral stalk and capsule of most liverworts. Mosses and liverworts have a characteristic "look" by which the beginner will soon learn to distinguish them, even in the field.

It is surprisingly easy to make and maintain a collection of liverworts, since they need neither to be pressed nor specially dried, and since they are not bothered by insect pests. The best procedure in collecting is to take everything that looks different, even though it will inevitably lead to much duplication, especially at first, because of the variability of species under different conditions. Liverworts may be collected at any season of the year, although they are most conspicuous and easily separated from their substratum just after a rain. A metal collecting can, or vasculum, may be used, but more convenient is a canvas bag or side pack about 8 by 12 inches. Such bags, equipped with a shoulder strap, are available at sporting goods stores. A large sharp knife is invaluable to scrape liverworts from stones and trees, or to shave off a thin layer of soil or rotten wood. Unnecessary soil must be avoided, as in a packet it crumbles to dust in which the specimens become lost. Specimens up to several square inches across are desirable, although sometimes only a very minute amount is available. Individual collections should be carefully separated from each other to avoid confusion and breakage. Several convenient and widely used methods are: (1) to place the specimens in folded paper packets or envelopes, (2) to roll or wrap them up in paper held in place with a rubber band, or (3) to put them in small (1 pound) paper bags. No matter what procedure is followed, a certain minimum amount of information must be written on the container at the time the specimen is collected. The habitat is important for identification. For example, so few liverworts grow in running water that a Michigan specimen from a brook through a cedar swamp is almost certainly *Chiloscyphus rivularis*. The substratum is also important, as it is usually necessary for identification. For liverworts growing on the bark of living trees, it is wise to identify the tree, as bark-inhabiting liverworts are apt to prefer one species of tree to another. The locality should be given as closely as can be ascertained, by section number and township, or by mileage on named roads, if no town or city is nearby. Official topographic maps and county road maps are extremely useful to collectors working in a reasonably small area. The date and the name of the collector are essential to well-authenticated specimens. The collector should also make as shrewd a guess as possible as to the name of the plant, because only in this way will he gradually come to know the species of liverworts in the field. Much of the effort of re-copying habitat and locality data may be prevented by carrying a field note book and giving each specimen a consecutive number, entering in the notebook only data unique to each specimen. General information on habitat and locality can then apply to a series of specimens from the same place.

In a permanent collection, the specimens are usually kept in folded paper packets. For example, the University of Michigan uses two sizes of paper packets, $3 \times 5\frac{1}{2}$ and $4 \times 5\frac{1}{2}$ inches, folded from a good grade of bond paper. In most large collections these packets are glued or pinned in two rows to standard herbarium sheets ($11\frac{1}{2} \times 16\frac{1}{2}$ inches), one species to each sheet. A small personal collection, in which each species is not represented by many specimens from different places, is best kept for ready reference and comparison of specimens in shoe boxes or filing cabinets, in alphabetical order. The name of the species and the collection data may be neatly written either on the outside of the packet or customarily on a special label pasted to the packet. The more information that the collector has printed on his label, such as his name and the locality from which his specimens came, the less he will have to fill in by hand.

How to Identify Liverworts

FOR IDENTIFICATION of the more common species of liverworts, neither laboratory nor technical equipment is needed. The first necessity is a good hand-lens, preferably of the triple aplanat type, with a magnification of 14x to 20x. Although such a lens is expensive, the flat field and clear image make it worthwhile. If a triplet lens cannot be afforded, then a Coddington or doublet lens will serve. Another absolute necessity is a very sharp pocket knife, or folding razor knife, or perhaps a smaller blade of the collecting knife recommended earlier, for cutting casual sections of thallose liverworts and other rough dissection of specimens. A small celluloid or wood ruler measuring both millimeters and inches is the final requirement.

Fresh plants are the easiest to study, although plants which have been dried for years will regain their green color and freshness if soaked for an instant in hot water. Many amateurs interested in liverworts collect specimens faster than they can be identified, and then catch up on the identifications during the winter months, when collecting is difficult.

In all the keys provided here, a series of choices must be made between progressively more minute but contrasting features or characters.

To use this key read both statements under numeral 1. Decide which description fits the specimen you are identifying. To the immediate right of the description selected you will observe an arabic numeral. Proceed to the point in the key where this numeral is found at the left of two alternate statements; giving no consideration to intervening numbers, once a choice has been made. Read these two statements and choose the one which describes your specimen. On the same line as the selected statement, at the right, is another numeral. Find the place in the key where this number is at the left of two descriptions. Choose the appropriate one, as before, and continue in this manner until after having made a choice you find a name at the right of the line of your selected description. This, if an error in judgment has not crept in, is the name of your specimen. Complete descriptions of all liverworts mentioned will be found at another point in the text by referring to the index.

In working a specimen through the key, any unfamiliar term or phrase must be looked up in the glossary (page 94) at once, because one mistake in following the key usually renders an identification completely impossible. Some liverworts which vary considerably and are consequently apt to be misinterpreted by the beginner have been included under both choices in the key. In case of doubt, a judicious "shopping around" among the illustrations and descriptions, as indicated by the references in the keys, often results in identification. It is suggested that, if opportunity offers, each liverwort be examined with a compound microscope, which will make obvious the details difficult to recognize with a hand-lens. Once this has been done, the species will be recognized easily thereafter with a hand-lens.

As soon as the student of liverworts has progressed beyond the scope of this elementary work, or needs further information, he is recommended to try his teeth on such useful technical works as Frye and Clark's "Hepaticae of North America" (University of Washington Publications in Biology, Volume 6, No. 1, 1937), of which only the first part has appeared; Macvicar's "The Student's Handbook of British Hepatics" (Wheldon & Wesley, London, England, 1926); and the numerous articles which have appeared in the forty-two volumes of "The Bryologist," the professional journal dealing with American mosses, liverworts, and lichens.

A Key to the Genera of Liverworts of Southern Michigan

1. Plant a flat, green thallus, circular or much elongated, without stem or leaves 2
   Plant distinctly consisting of a leafy stem 15
2. Thallus consisting, in cross section, of a solid, colorless to purple lower tissue and a green upper tissue containing air chambers which open to the upper surface by means of usually conspicuous pores (Pls. 1-3) 3
   Thallus consisting, in cross section, of green cells, all of which are more or less alike; without air chambers or pores 11
3. Thallus free-floating on or in the water 4
   Thallus not free-floating (although sometimes in very wet places), but firmly attached to the substratum 5
4. Thallus narrow, ribbon-like, rarely reaching 1 mm. in width; without scales on the lower side; floating just under the surface of the water ...... *Riccia fluitans*
   Thallus butterfly- or heart-shaped, 2-8 mm. wide, the lower side covered with red or purple scales; floating on the very surface of the water (Frontispiece) .... *Ricciocarpus natans*
5. Thallus narrow, 3 mm. or less wide, growing on the muddy bottom of dried-up pools 6
   Thallus at least 4 mm. wide 7
6. Thallus 1 mm. or less in width, without a furrow along the middle .... *Riccia fluitans*
   Thallus 2-3 mm. wide, with a furrow along the middle .... *Ricciocarpus natans*
7. Thallus bearing special cup-like or crescent-shaped depressions filled with flat, circular gemmae (Pl. 3) 8
   Thallus without special structures filled with circular gemmae 9
8. Gemma-filled receptacles crescent-shaped, not fringed; a greenhouse weed not growing out-of-doors (Pl. 3, fig. 2) .... *Lunularia cruciata*
   Gemma-filled receptacles cup-like, fringed; plants growing out-of-doors as well as in greenhouses (Pl. 3, fig. 1) .... *Marchantia polymorpha*
9. Thallus, in cross section, showing several layers of air chambers; archegonial receptacle with 4-6 lobes (Pl. 1, fig. 2) .... *Reboulia hemisphaerica*
   Thallus, in cross section, showing a single layer of air chambers; archegonial receptacle without well-defined lobes 10
10. Upper side of thallus with a conspicuous netted pattern, corresponding to the diamond-shaped air chamber within, each diamond with a large white pore in the center; the pore one layer of cells thick at the opening; living plants with a spicy fragrance; archegonial receptacle conical (Pl. 1, fig. 1; Pl. 2, figs. 3, 4) .... *Conocephalum conicum*

Diamond-shaped pattern on upper side of thallus not at all conspicuous; pore barrel-shaped in section, surrounded by several layers of cells; archegonial receptacle flat, with a cross- or star-shaped raised area on the upper surface..*Preissia quadrata*

---

11. Thallus ribbon-like or heart-shaped, never circular, although, with its branches, it may form an approximately circular colony (Pls. 4, 5).........12

    Thallus circular or nearly so; elongated, horn-like sporophytes usually present (Pl. 22)..47

12. Thallus one layer of cells thick except for the much thicker and well-defined midrib (Pl. 5, fig. 6)..*Pallavicinia Lyellii*

    Thallus of more than one layer of cells in thickness, at least in the middle; without a well-defined midrib..13

13. Thallus less than 2 mm. wide (Pl. 4, figs. 3-8).................................*Riccardia*

    Thallus more than 2 mm. broad...14

14. Thallus long and ribbon-like, bright bluish-green, with a greasy or oily surface (Pl. 4, figs. 1, 2)..*Riccardia pinguis*

    Thallus heart-shaped, clear green or with a tinge of red; never appearing oily or greasy (Pl. 5, figs. 1-5)..*Pellia epiphylla*

---

15. Leaves without a smaller, infolded lower lobe..16

    Leaves with a smaller lobe folded against the much larger (except in *Scapania*) upper lobe (Pls. 19-21)...42

16. Leaves variously toothed, lobed or divided...17

    Leaves undivided and without any sort of marginal teeth..........................34

17. Leaves deeply divided into, or fringed with, hair-like teeth (Pl. 6; Pl. 7, figs. 1-4)..18

    Leaves toothed at the margin, or 2-4 lobed, but neither fringed nor deeply dissected...20

18. Leaves divided to base into 3-4 thread-like teeth; a delicate species growing on moist soil, humus, or rotten wood (Pl. 7, figs. 1-4)...*Blepharostoma trichophyllum*

    Leaves densely fringed along the margin with hair-like teeth; plants larger (Pl. 6)..19

19. Plants large, pale green or yellowish, regularly pinnately branched; growing on the ground in swampy woods (Pl. 6, figs. 1-3).......*Trichocolea tomentella*

    Plants brownish-green or reddish; growing on rotten wood, commonly in dry places (Pl. 6, figs. 4, 5)..*Ptilidium pulcherrimum*

20. Leaves incubous: the upper margin of one leaf overlapping the base of the leaf next above; all with underleaves (Pl. 7, fig. 6; Pl. 9, figs. 1, 4)........21
    Leaves succubous: the lower margin of one leaf overlapping the upper part of the leaf next below; underleaves present or absent........23
21. Leaves divided about half their length into 4 teeth or lobes which curve downward (Pl. 8, figs. 1-4)........*Lepidozia reptans*
    Leaves divided much less than half their length into 2 or 3 lobes or teeth.....22
22. Plants large, dark green; leaves 3-toothed at the apex (Pl. 7, figs. 5, 6)
    ....*Bazzania trilobata*
    Plants pale green, very flat on the substratum; leaves only obscurely notched at the very apex, much more commonly without teeth (Pl. 8, figs. 5-8)........*Calypogeia*

23. Underleaves present, commonly conspicuous, leaves 2-lobed........24
    Underleaves absent or invisible with a hand-lens........28
24. Underleaves simple, neither divided nor toothed........25
    Underleaves divided into two long, slender, sharp lobes, which in turn may be toothed........26
25. Plant growing on rotten wood; lobes of leaf sharp (Pl. 10, figs. 8-12)........
    ....*Harpanthus scutatus*
    Plant growing in bogs on peat moss; lobes of leaf blunt (Pl. 14, figs. 10-13)
    ....*Cladopodiella fluitans*
26. Divisions of underleaf not at all toothed; plants yellowish-green, with a greasy, opaque appearance (Pl. 10, figs. 6, 7)........*Geocalyx graveolens*
    Divisions of underleaf with a supplementary tooth at the side; plants pale green, appearing transparent........27
27. Perianth at the end of the stem or a main branch, conspicuously 3-angled (Pl. 12, figs. 4-8)........*Lophocolea*
    Perianth on a very short lateral branch, appearing to come from the side of the stem, not conspicuously 3-angled (Pl. 12, fig. 3)........*Chiloscyphus*
28. Leaves with many (more than 10) small, sharp teeth regularly arranged around the margin; not at all lobed (Pl. 18, figs. 1, 2)........
    ....*Plagiochila asplenioides*
    Leaves with no more than 4 lobes or teeth at the apex........29
29. Leaves regularly notched at the apex, with 2-4 lobes or teeth........30
    Leaves irregularly lobed and toothed; plants very small, pale green; sporophytes produced in groups of 2 or more along the stem (Pl. 5, figs. 7-8)
    ....*Fossombronia cristula*

30. Leaves 4-lobed (Pl. 15, figs. 4, 5) ....*Barbilophozia barbata*
    Leaves 2-lobed (Pls. 13, 14) 31
31. Leaf lobes blunt (Pl. 14, figs. 10-13) ....*Cladopodiella fluitans*
    Leaf lobes acute 32
32. Leaves very concave, the lower lobe with a sac-like swelling; both lobes ending in long, slender, curved points (Pl. 13, figs. 1-3) ...*Nowellia curvifolia*
    Leaf lobes neither with sac-like swellings, nor ending in hair points 33
33. Leaves oval to circular, always wider than the stem, the lobes pointing toward each other, and actually crossing each other in one species (Pls. 13, 14) ....*Cephalozia*
    Leaves not circular, narrower than the stem in sterile plants, the lobes divergent; extremely small plants, almost invisible to the naked eye (Pl. 10, figs. 1-5) ....*Cephaloziella*

---

34. Leaves incubous: the upper margin of one leaf overlapping the base of the leaf next above; underleaves present (Pl. 8, figs. 5-8; Pl. 9) ....*Calypogeia*
    Leaves succubous: the lower margin of one leaf overlapping the upper part of the leaf next below; underleaves present or absent 35
35. Underleaves present 36
    Underleaves absent, or invisible with a hand-lens 38
36. Underleaves deeply divided into 2 lobes (Pl. 11; Pl. 12, figs. 1-3) ....
    ....*Chiloscyphus*
    Underleaves simple, not divided in any manner 37
37. Large plants with circular lower leaves and pointed upper leaves which bear gemmae on their margins; growing in bogs among peat mosses (Pl. 17, figs. 5, 6) ....*Mylia anomala*
    Small plants with circular leaves throughout; gemmae not produced at the edge of the leaf but at the end of much drawn-out, erect branches; growing on humus and rotten wood (Pl. 18, figs. 3-5) ...*Odontoschisma denudatum*
38. Plants growing on moist soil, humus, rotten wood or shaded boulders; perianth not spindle-shaped 39
    Small liverworts growing on rocks kept continuously moist by a trickle of running water or by spray; perianth spindle-shaped (Pl. 16, figs. 1, 2; Pl. 17, figs. 1-4) 41
39. Basal edge of leaf folded sharply back, toward the lower side (Pl. 18, figs. 1, 2) ....*Plagiochila asplenioides*
    Basal edge of leaf flat, not at all folded back 40

40. Leaves surrounding the perianth like the other leaves; perianth tubular, suddenly contracted to a beaked mouth (Pl. 16, figs. 3, 4) .... *Jungermannia lanceolata*

    Leaves surrounding the perianth fringed along the lower margin; perianth ovate, not suddenly contracted to the mouth, which is fringed with long teeth (Pl. 15, figs. 1-3) .... *Jamesoniella autumnalis*

41. Base of perianth fused to the upper leaves; plants pale green with a reddish tinge (Pl. 17, figs. 1-4) .... *Plectocolea hyalina*

    Base of perianth not united to upper leaves; plants dark green (Pl. 16, figs. 1, 2) .... *Jungermannia pumila*

---

42 Underleaves absent 43

    Underleaves present, usually conspicuous 45

43. Lower lobe of leaf much larger than upper lobe; leaf margin with numerous small, sharp teeth (Pl. 19, figs. 1-6) .... *Scapania nemorosa*

    Lower lobe of leaf much smaller than upper lobe; leaf margin without teeth of any kind 44

44. Upper leaf lobe rounded, usually bearing disc-shaped gemmae on its margin; cells smooth (Pl. 19, figs. 7-9) .... *Radula complanata*

    Upper lobe with an acute point; cells bearing small spine-like projections; extremely small plants (Pl. 20, figs. 3-7) .... *Cololejeunea Biddlecomiae*

45. Underleaf not notched; plants very large, dark green (Pl. 20, figs. 1, 2) .... *Porella platyphylloidea*

    Underleaf nearly circular, deeply notched 46

46. Plants very small, blackish or reddish-green, growing well up on the trunks of living trees; lower lobe of leaf helmet shaped, sac-like (Pl. 21) ...... *Frullania*

    Plants pale green, on the base of trees or on rocks, lower lobe of leaf neither helmet shaped nor saccate (Pl. 20, figs. 8-11) ...... *Lejeunea cavifolia*

---

47. Sporophyte 1-3 cm. long, threadlike, splitting into 2 parts (Pl. 22, figs. 4-6) .... *Anthoceros laevis*

    Sporophyte spindle-shaped, about 1 mm. long, almost completely enveloped in a tubular outgrowth of the thallus (Pl. 22, figs. 1-3) .... *Notothylas orbicularis*

The Liverworts of Southern Michigan

Riccia L.

Thallus growing on the ground or floating in fresh water; branching dichotomously; of two layers: a thin, colorless basal region and an upper green region containing narrow air spaces between vertical columns of cells, or much larger air chambers which result in a spongy tissue, the pores very inconspicuous, as the epidermal cells surrounding them are unmodified. Sporophyte spherical, its wall one layer of cells thick throughout, soon decaying away, releasing the dark spores which have no specialized sterile cells among them. Named in honor of P. F. Ricci, an Italian botanist.

Although twenty species of *Riccia* are known in the United States and Canada, only one of them has been recognized in Michigan. Since several species are known in Ohio and Indiana, careful search of appropriate habitats, such as moist clay in fields and gardens, the crevices in brick sidewalks, etc., especially in the southernmost tiers of counties, should result in the addition of at least one species of *Riccia* to the flora of Michigan.

Riccia fluitans L.

This little liverwort floats just below the surface of standing water in marshes, ponds and pools. The narrow, ribbon-like thallus, which is 0.5-1.0 mm. wide and 1-3 cm. long, forks at regular intervals, the branches spreading nearly at right angles. As the result of rapid growth and repeated forking, the plants usually become matted together into firm, yellowish-green, floating balls which may reach six inches or more in diameter. During the summer, when the water level of the pond falls, the plants are stranded along the shore and grow out over the mud and dead leaves. In such a habitat the plants are very little different from the floating form, except that thick mats or balls are never formed, but only a thin green film. Sporophytes are extremely uncommon in this liverwort, at least in Michigan, and occur only in the stranded plants; floating plants are always sterile. In autumn the floating plants sink to the bottom, where they winter over. With the stranded plants, which become submerged in late fall as the ponds refill, they are protected from too severe cold by the water, whose temperature does not fall far below freezing. In the spring, as the temperature of the water rises and the days become longer, the submerged plants regain their activity and float to the surface.

The thread- or ribbon-like appearance of this liverwort, its lack of rhizoids or rootlets, and its aquaric habitat combine to cause it to be too often taken for an alga, especially the water net *(Hydrodictyon)* or *Nitella*. It is also confused with species of *Lemna,* a genus of very small, aquatic flowering plants.

The rapid growth and bright yellowish-green color of *Riccia fluitans* should make it a popular plant for aquaria.

RICCIOCARPUS Corda

Thallus usually floating in fresh water, more rarely growing attached on wet soil; branching dichotomously; heart-shaped or butterfly-shaped; consisting of two layers, a very thin, usually colored, solid basal region of which the lower side produces numerous, conspicuous red to purplish-black scales, and an upper thick, spongy layer composed almost entirely of several layers of large air chambers which are separated by walls only one layer of cells thick, the uppermost layer of chambers visible through the thin, transparent epidermis, and opening through it to the air by means of small pores. The terrestrial form is much more branched, its branches narrower, ribbon-like; scales very inconspicuous. Sporophyte spherical, black when mature, contained within the much enlarged archegonium, its wall one layer of cells thick, finally decaying as the thallus decays, to release the black, rough spores, which are not accompanied by specialized sterile cells or elaters. Name from *Riccia* and Greek *carpos,* fruit, in reference to the conspicuous black sporophytes.

The single species of *Ricciocarpus* is widely distributed through the temperate and subtropical parts of the world, being known from every continent.

RICCIOCARPUS NATANS (L.) Corda
Frontispiece

Through June and July, large numbers of this silvery green, heart-shaped or butterfly-shaped liverwort cover the surface of many shallow ponds and pools, especially those which are shaded by the button bush (*Cephalanthus*). Unlike *Riccia fluitans*, which grows just below the surface of the water, this plant floats on the surface and exposes its whole upper side to the air. A casual section made with a sharp pocket knife and examined with a hand-lens will show the reason: nearly the whole thallus of *Ricciocarpus* is made up of buoyant air chambers, each surrounded by a thin layer of cells. Although this liverwort becomes stranded on the edges and bottom of the pool when the water level falls, it behaves very differently from *Riccia fluitans*. In the first place, the plants continue active growth and branching on the moist mud and humus, but since the branches cannot break off and float away as new butterfly-shaped individuals, as they do on the aquatic form, a very different manner of growth results. It took many years for botanists to realize that one liverwort could have two such dissimilar growth forms, which for a long time had been considered as separate species. Furthermore, in striking contrast to *Riccia fluitans*, the terrestrial form of this liverwort never produces sporophytes, whereas the floating form produces them abundantly. During June, most floating plants roughly sectioned to observe the air chambers, will also be seen to contain the black, spherical sporophytes embedded in the green tissue. Each mature sporophyte is completely filled with black, spiny spores.

This species is most often mistaken for one of the duckweeds (*Spiro-*

EXPLANATION OF PLATE 1

Fig. 1, Conocephalum conicum X2: thallus with two archegonial receptacles, one extended and one sessile; Fig. 2, Reboulia hemisphaerica X5: thallus with three archegonial receptacles; Figs. 3-4, Marchantia polymorpha: 3, thallus with four antheridial receptacles X3, 4, thallus with three archegonial receptacles X2.

Photographs by Dr. E. B. Mains

PLATE 1

PLATE 2 [26] *Photographs by Dr. E. B. Mair*

dela and *Lemna)* with which it is often associated, but differs in its larger size, spongy structure and enclosed fruits.

Ricciocarpus is an interesting and unusual aquarium plant, and grows well on shaded, covered surfaces.

REBOULIA Raddi

Thallus never aquatic, branching dichotomously; also producing new lateral branches from the apex; air chambers showing very indistinctly through the epidermis, irregularly divided by supplementary partitions, and so appearing to be in more than one layer, containing no green filaments, opening to the surface by simple pores. Male receptacle sessile; archegonial receptacle hemispherical, distinctly lobed, on a stalk 2-3 cm. long; sporophyte consisting of a foot, a short seta, and a subglobose capsule which splits open rather irregularly at the apex and releases the rough spores and the elaters. Named in honor of E. de Reboul, an Italian botanist.

The solitary species of *Reboulia* is even more widely distributed over the world than *Ricciocarpus natans*.

REBOULIA HEMISPHAERICA (L.) Raddi
Plate 1, Figure 2; Plate 2, Figure 2

The preference of this liverwort for steep, shaded hillsides, whether of earth or rock, and its ability to withstand more drying than the other members of the family Marchantiaceae in Michigan will help in identifying it. A steep earth bank in the woods, in an open meadow, or in a ravine is a likely habitat for this species, which never grows very close to water, much less in it. On the calcareous sandstone cliffs along the river at Grand Ledge is the most luxuriant growth of this liverwort I

EXPLANATION OF PLATE 2

Fig. 1, Marchantia polymorpha X5: underside of archegonial receptacle; Fig. 2, Reboulia hemisphaerica X15: underside of archegonial receptacle; Figs. 3-4, Conocephalum conicum X10: 3, archegonial receptacle with young sporophytes, 4, archegonial receptacle with older sporophytes.

have seen in Michigan. From these cliffs came the specimens whose photographs appear here.

The ribbon-like thallus is 5-7 mm. wide and 1-4 cm. long, light dusty green, usually with purplish margins and lower side, the margins curling inward when the plant is dry. In June and July, when the plants bear the characteristic lobed archegonial receptacle, there is no danger of confusing this liverwort with any other. Sterile plants may be more puzzling, however, and need to be studied more carefully. Examination of a thin cross section made with a sharp razor blade or pocket knife will show the upper part of the thallus to be composed of a spongy tissue containing several layers of air chambers. The pores by which the uppermost air chambers open to the outside are surrounded by a ring of cells one layer in thickness.

A related liverwort, *Asterella tenella,* will eventually be discovered in southern Michigan, since it has been collected across the Detroit River, at Windsor. It grows in about the same habitat as *Reboulia,* but has a curious and beautiful white or reddish basket-like fringe around each sporophyte.

CONOCEPHALUM Web.

Thallus large, perennial, branching dichotomously. Air chambers in one layer, their boundaries showing conspicuously as rhombic areas on the upper epidermis, filled with crowded green filaments whose end cell is pear shaped, especially near the pores; pores simple, surrounded by 5-7 radiating rows of cells raised to the opening. Antheridial receptacle sessile; female receptacle obtusely conical, hardly lobed, its stalk pale, 3-8 cm. long. Sporophyte consisting of foot, a relatively long seta, and an ellipsoidal capsule which opens by the throwing off of an apical cap. Name from Greek *conos,* a cone, and *cephale,* a head, from the conical female receptacle.

Two species of *Conocephalum* are recognized, but only the following is native to North America.

Conocephalum conicum (L.) Dumort.
Plate 1, Figure 1; Plate 2, Figures 3, 4

This conspicuous liverwort is probably the most common one throughout the state. It forms extensive silvery green carpets on moist soil and rocks, especially along streams and in swampy places, but rarely grows actually in the water. Although it is often confused with *Marchantia polymorpha*, it may be separated easily, after a little experience, by its much more apparent network of larger, diamond-shaped air chambers, each with a conspicuous white pore in its exact center (Pl. 1, fig. 1). Also, *Conocephalum* lacks completely the cups filled with flat reproductive buds or gemmae so characteristic of *Marchantia*. Very curiously, the easiest and most certain means of recognizing *Conocephalum* in the field is unfamiliar to most botanists: the odor. When crushed, the plants yield a pungent, spicy aroma somewhat resembling a mixture of cloves and cinnamon.

From late fall to early spring, the stalk of the female receptacle is very short, and as a result the cone-shaped head remains seated at the apex of the thallus (Pl. 1, fig. 1, at right). With the coming of the first warm weather, the stalk suddenly begins to elongate very rapidly and within a few days has raised the female receptacle several centimeters above the ground (Pl. 1, fig. 1, center; Pl. 2, figs. 3, 4). After the spores are shed, the colorless stalk dries up and very soon disappears. Because the spores of *Conocephalum* are usually shed before the earliest spring flowers bloom and because of the short time elapsing between the elongation of the stalk and the disappearance of the fruit, very few people are acquainted with this liverwort in its full fruiting condition.

Lunularia Adans.

Thallus perennial in greenhouses but not hardy out-of-doors in our climate, branching dichotomously and by new growth from the apex of old branches. Discoid gemmae, or special buds for propagation produced in crescent-shaped depressions on the upper surface. Air chambers in one layer, their floor crowded with short, erect, green filaments; each chamber with a simple, raised pore. Antheridial receptacles, female receptacles, and sporophytes never produced in our region; in fact, they have been reported only once from North America, from California. Name from Latin *lunularis,* like a little moon, from the crescentic gemma cups.

The single species of this genus has a worldwide distribution. Like the next species, it owes much of its spread to man's activities, and so its original natural distribution cannot now be determined.

LUNULARIA CRUCIATA (L.) Dumort.
Plate 3, Figure 1

Although this handsome liverwort occurs in Michigan only as a greenhouse weed, it is common enough to merit consideration here. It grows exceedingly rapidly, soon producing green or yellowish-green mats which may completely cover the surface of pots and benches in greenhouses and conservatories. The esteem in which this liverwort is held in some quarters is illustrated by the experience of one of my students who asked a florist in central Michigan if she might look around in his greenhouse for liverworts. The florist was so indignant at her suspicion that he might be harboring such weeds, that he refused her admission to the greenhouse for any purpose. Not all florists are quite so positive in their prejudice against *Lunularia* and some of them, in fact, encourage or at least tolerate it as a decorative ground cover under the benches. However, the subject of collecting *Lunularia* (or *Marchantia*) in commercial greenhouses should be approached circumspectly!

Although this species is always sterile in greenhouses, it may be recognized at once by the short, wide thallus, which always bears the unique crescent-shaped ridge sheltering a depression filled with flat, disc-like gemmae (Pl. 3, fig. 1). Each gemma is able to grow at once into a

EXPLANATION OF PLATE 3
Fig. 1, Lunularia cruciata X5: thallus with gemmae; Fig. 2, Marchantia polymorpha X5: thallus with gemmae.

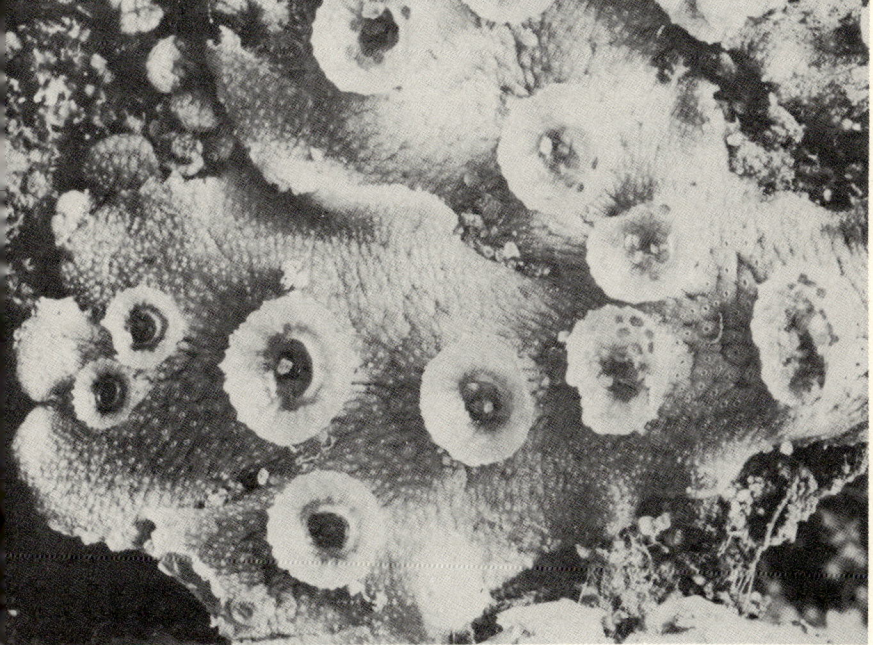

Photographs by Dr. E. B. Mains

PLATE 3

PLATE 4 [32]

new green plant, under favorable conditions, and the large number of gemmae which are produced by one plant explains the rapid spread of this liverwort in greenhouses.

MARCHANTIA L.

Thallus perennial, dichotomously branched; bearing discoid gemmae on its upper surface in small, fringed, goblet-shaped cups; its air chambers in one layer, their boundaries well marked on the upper surface as polygonal areas clearly visible, but neither as large nor as conspicuous as in *Conocephalum*, their floor covered with crowded, branching green filaments. Pores hardly visible to the naked eye, barrel-shaped in section, surrounded by 3-6 circles of superimposed cells. Male receptacle stalked, flat on top, round or indistinctly lobed; female receptacle long-stalked, distinctly and deeply 7-9 lobed; sporophyte consisting of a foot, a short seta and a subglobose capsule which splits irregularly, allowing the nearly smooth, bright yellow spores to escape. Named in honor of N. Marchant, a French botanist.

Of the three species of *Marchantia* known in the United States and Canada, only one is known in Michigan. It, however, is probably the most widely distributed hepatic in the world, and ranges in North America from beyond the Arctic Circle into tropical Central America.

MARCHANTIA POLYMORPHA L.
Plate 1, Figures 3, 4; Plate 2, Figure 1; Plate 3, Figure 2

This, the largest of our liverworts, is a common weed, both out-of-doors and in greenhouses. Man is apparently the most important agent in its dispersal, since its growth is most luxuriant in gardens, around habitations, and especially on ground where wood has been burned. The

---

EXPLANATION OF PLATE 4

Figs. 1-2, Riccardia pinguis X5; Figs. 3-4, Riccardia multifida X10; Figs. 5-8, Riccardia latifrons X10.

site of an old wood fire will nearly always develop a fine cover of *Marchantia,* which is usually accompanied by the weedy moss *Funaria hygrometrica* Hedw. The year after a fire had devastated many acres of bog forest at Mud Lake, north of Ann Arbor, *Marchantia polymorpha* covered nearly the whole burn, and was the dominant plant until larger plants gradually crowded it out.

Marchantia differs strongly from the other thallose liverworts in several respects. Most plants are characterized by either the flat, round, antheridial receptacles on short stalks (Pl. 1, fig. 3), or the stalked female receptacle curiously lobed like the ribs of an umbrella (Pl. 1, fig. 4; Pl. 2, fig. 1). Sterile plants may usually be distinguished by the little fringed cups filled with disc-shaped gemmae (Pl. 3, fig. 2). The occasional specimens of *Marchantia* which lack all reproductive structures, even the gemmae-cups, may be distinguished from *Conocephalum* by the less distinct network of air chambers, whose pores are more difficult to see with the naked eye. A certain identification can always be made from a thin cross section of the thallus, in which compound pores, surrounded by a barrel-shaped ring of cells several layers thick, may be seen with a good lens.

Preissia Corda

Thallus branching dichotomously or through new growth at the apex. Air chambers in a single layer, not subdivided by supplementary partitions, their floor covered with vertical, usually branching, green filaments; pores barrel-shaped, surrounded by 4-5 superimposed cells. Antheridial receptacle discoid, on a stalk about 1 cm. long; female receptacle discoid, round or shallowly lobed, with 3-5 (usually 4) radiating ridges on the nearly flat upper side, its stalk 5-10 cm. long. Capsule nearly spherical, opening irregularly. Named in honor of B. Preiss, a Bohemian naturalist.

The solitary species of *Preissia* is widely distributed in the colder parts of the Northern Hemisphere.

Preissia quadrata (Scop.) Nees

Although this species is most common in the northern part of Michigan, especially in the Upper Peninsula, it has also been found in our area at Grand Ledge, near Kalamazoo, and at Port Austin. A careful search will undoubtedly uncover other localities in southern Michigan. It grows on moist calcareous soil and rotten logs along streams, very close to the water, and on moist rocks. On the rocky shores of Lake Superior and at the tip of the "thumb" in Lake Huron, it grows on sandstone cliffs within reach of the waves.

The plants, which are a pale, dusty green, with reddish or purple margins, spread into circular patches from a common center, especially upon rock. The stalked archegonial receptacles develop in June and July, whereas the antheridial receptacles, with much shorter stalks, reach maturity in August and September. The only species with which *Preissia* is likely to be confused, when sterile, is *Reboulia hemisphaerica,* from which it is to be distinguished by its preference for a much moister habitat, and the disposition of the air chambers in one layer, not in a spongy region several layers thick. The final and most conclusive character, but one which requires a good lens and patient sectioning to demonstrate, is the presence in each air chamber of a compound or barrel-shaped pore, whose limiting cells are in several layers. The only other Michigan liverwort possessing this feature is *Marchantia polymorpha,* which is larger, grows usually in a different habitat, and generally produces its characteristic gemma cups.

Riccardia S. F. Gray

Thallus slightly branched to regularly pinnate, fleshy, several layers of cells thick, lens-shaped to elliptic in cross section, a narrow margin one layer of cells thick present in some species; interior cells usually somewhat larger than the epidermal cells, otherwise no cell modification, and with no trace either of air chambers or pores. Antheridia produced on short lateral branches; archegonia on a short branch originally lateral but which appears ventral through later growth of the thallus. Sporophyte surrounded until maturity by the large, cylindrical, modified archegonium or calyptra, through which the ripe capsule bursts as the result of growth of the long seta. The capsule splits open by four regular valves which bear at their free end a tuft of attached hairs, the elater bearers. When the capsule opens, these threads help scatter the spores. Named originally "Riccardius" by S. F. Gray, probably in honor of some friend.

Of the six species found in the United States and Canada (as well as in Europe), three occur within our range.

Key to the species of *Riccardia*

1. Thallus 3-10 mm. wide, 10-15 cells thick at its thickest part............................*Riccardia pinguis*
   Thallus 2 mm. or less in width, less than 10 cells thick at the thickest part... 2
2. Plants regularly and pinnately branched, unistratose margin of the smaller branches 2-3 cells wide..............................*Riccardia multifida*
   Plants irregularly or palmately branched, unistratose margin of the smaller branches 1 cell wide or lacking..............................*Riccardia latifrons*

Riccardia pinguis (L.) S. F. Gray
Plate 4, Figures 1, 2

At the base of cattail plants, especially on the floating mat around bog lakes, one will find this liverwort. It grows also on the ground in ditches, in arbor vitae swamps, and very rarely on rotten wood. The plants are dark bluish-green, becoming nearly black when dry, and have a curious oily or greasy lustre which is unique to this largest member of the genus. The narrow, strap-shaped thallus, which is 3-10 mm. broad and 2-5 cm. long, branches slightly and irregularly. When fresh, the plants are very brittle and fragile, breaking easily in the process of collection. The fleshy thallus, which becomes gradually thicker toward the center, distinguishes this liverwort from all others in Michigan, and the large size separates it from the other species of *Riccardia*.

RICCARDIA MULTIFIDA (L.) S. F. Gray
Plate 4, Figures 3, 4

In southern Michigan this delicate little liverwort grows most commonly in deep arbor vitae swamps, either directly on wet ground or on rotten wood. The regular branching, twice (or more) pinnate, and the more or less transparent margin one cell thick and 2-3 cells wide on the smaller thallus branches are the distinguishing features of this graceful but inconspicuous liverwort, whose branches are usually less than 0.5 mm. wide. Because of their small size, this species and the next are commonly overlooked.

RICCARDIA LATIFRONS Lindb.
Plate 4, Figures 5-8

On rotten wood, especially old stumps and half-submerged logs in swampy woods, occurs this small, bluish-green liverwort. It differs from *Riccardia pinguis* in the more numerous, palmate branches, which are often very irregular. The thallus is larger than that of the preceding, reaching nearly 2 mm. in width, but is still much smaller than *Riccardia pinguis*. In Michigan, at least, this species usually occurs as a few individuals scattered among mosses or among other liverworts and only rarely in any quantity. Hence most collectors do not find it.

PALLAVICINIA S. F. Gray

Thallus ribbon-like, 3-8 cm. long, to 4 mm. wide, of a delicate texture, one layer of cells thick, except for the conspicuous, much thickened midrib with a central strand of long, narrow, thickened cells. Antheridia on the much narrower male plants; archegonia in groups on the upper side of the midrib, surrounded by a cup-like fringe, the involucre; the sporophyte enclosed until maturity not only in the modified archegonium or calyptra, but also in a tubular protective sheath, the pseudoperianth, which buds out from the thallus. The ripe capsule is cylindrical, and bursts through both the calyptra and the pseudoperianth by

PLATE 5 [38]

a rapid development of the long, colorless seta. Originally named "Pallavicinius" by S. F. Gray, probably in honor of some friend.

Only one species of this genus, as interpreted at present, is recognized in North America north of Mexico, but it has, also, a worldwide distribution.

PALLAVICINIA LYELLII (Hook.) S. F. Gray
Plate 5, Figure 6

This handsome liverwort, which is more common in the western half of southern Michigan, grows in extensive mats over bare earth in wet places, such as sandy stream banks and in arbor vitae swamps. The long, ribbon-like thallus, with a conspicuous midrib, makes it easy to recognize, and to distinguish from *Pellia* and *Riccardia,* both of which lack a midrib. Furthermore, the curious cup-like fringes, or involucres, at regular intervals on the upper surface of female plants are unmistakable. Even in the absence of mature sporophytes, the involucres can be seen easily.

PELLIA Raddi

Thallus branching dichotomously, with a wide, indistinct midrib which gradually merges in the margin or wing where this is only one layer of cells in thickness; rootlets or rhizoids numerous, produced from the underside of the midrib, which appear to the naked eye as tiny bubbles; archegonia in groups of 4-12, in special cup-like or pocket-like cavities opening toward the front of the thallus; capsule spherical, extended on a very long seta when mature, opening by 4 regular valves; special threads or elater bearers attached to the inner base of the capsule help to disseminate the many celled spores (Pl. 5, figs. 4, 5). Named in honor of L. Pelli-Fabbroni, of Florence, a friend of Raddi.

EXPLANATION OF PLATE 5

Figs. 1-5, Pellia epiphylla X5: 1-2, thallus with young sporophytes within the involucre, 3-5, progressive stages in the opening of the capsule, showing fixed elaters; Fig. 6, Pallavicinia Lyellii X5: thallus with involucres, pseudoperianths, and one capsule on an elongating seta; Figs. 7-8, Fossombronia cristula X10: plants with young sporophytes within the involucre.

Pellia epiphylla (L.) Corda
Plate 5, Figures 1-5

In northern Michigan this species grows on soil, rotten wood, and all over the moist cliffs along the south shore of Lake Superior, but in our range it is restricted to very wet places, as swamps and bogs, and especially the floating cattail mats around bog lakes. Whatever the habitat, however, this species turns from bright or dark green to a deep purplish-red at the first frost. The very broad (5-15 mm.), thin, somewhat heart-shaped thallus is like no other liverwort which occurs here. The domed roof of the antheridial cavities is clearly visible to the naked eye (Fig. 2), but still more characteristic is the pocket- or pouch-like cavity or involucre which opens toward the growing point of the thallus and which contains the archegonia and then the sporophytes (Figs. 1-3). This liverwort differs from *Riccardia pinguis,* with which it commonly grows and is just as commonly confused, in the wider, thinner thallus, the dorsal (not lateral) antheridia and archegonia, the spherical capsule, and the large, many-celled spores. Both species grow very well and even fruit in terraria, to which they add much interest.

Fossombronia Raddi

Plants prostrate, attached firmly to the substratum by means of rhizoids, which are violet in most species; leaves in two rows, overlapping from apex to base of stem, margins irregularly ruffled, toothed, or lobed. Antheridia orange-yellow, on the upper side of the stem, naked or partly covered by special leaves; archegonia produced on the upper side of the stem, not ending its growth, the functional archegonia always near the tip of the stem, becoming enclosed in a large, bell-shaped sheath, the pseudoperianth, which is fringed or ruffled. Capsule spherical, on a short seta, opening somewhat irregularly. The large spores are characteristically ornamented in each species, and as all the species are very similar in vegetative structure, the spores and elaters form the most certain means of identification, but require the use of a microscope. Named in honor of V. Fossombroni, an influential Italian statesman.

Of the dozen species of *Fossombronia* in the United States and Canada, only one is known to occur in our range.

Fossombronia cristula Aust.
Plate 5, Figures 7, 8

This rare and delicate little liverwort should perhaps not be included here, since it has been collected only once in Michigan. However, its discovery at Paw Paw by Mr. H. R. Becker was reasonably recent (1935) and it is certain that directed search will turn up other localities for it. The genus is of unusual interest because it seems to bridge the gap between the thallose Jungermanniales Anacrogynae, in which archegonia are produced periodically on the same stem, and the leafy Jungermanniales Acrogynae, in which the archegonia develop at the tip of the stem and terminate its growth. *Fossombronia* characteristically produces progressively older sporophytes, often in groups (Figs. 7, 8), at intervals along the same stem, as does *Pallavicinia,* for example.

Fossombronia cristula is to be distinguished from other members of its genus by the small, rudimentary elaters. It was long known in the sand dunes of Indiana, close to the Michigan line, before Mr. Becker found it on peaty soil along the shore of Three Mile Lake, at Paw Paw, and will without doubt be found elsewhere in southern Michigan. The plants are very small, about 5 mm. long, never more than 10 mm., and a pale yellowish-green. When dry, the leaves assume an iridescent lustre apparent under a lens.

Ptilidium Nees

Plants prostrate, or tufted and erect, branched once or twice pinnately; leaves overlapping from base to apex of stem, deeply lobed, their whole margin finely and beautifully fringed with long, hair-like

PLATE 6 [42]

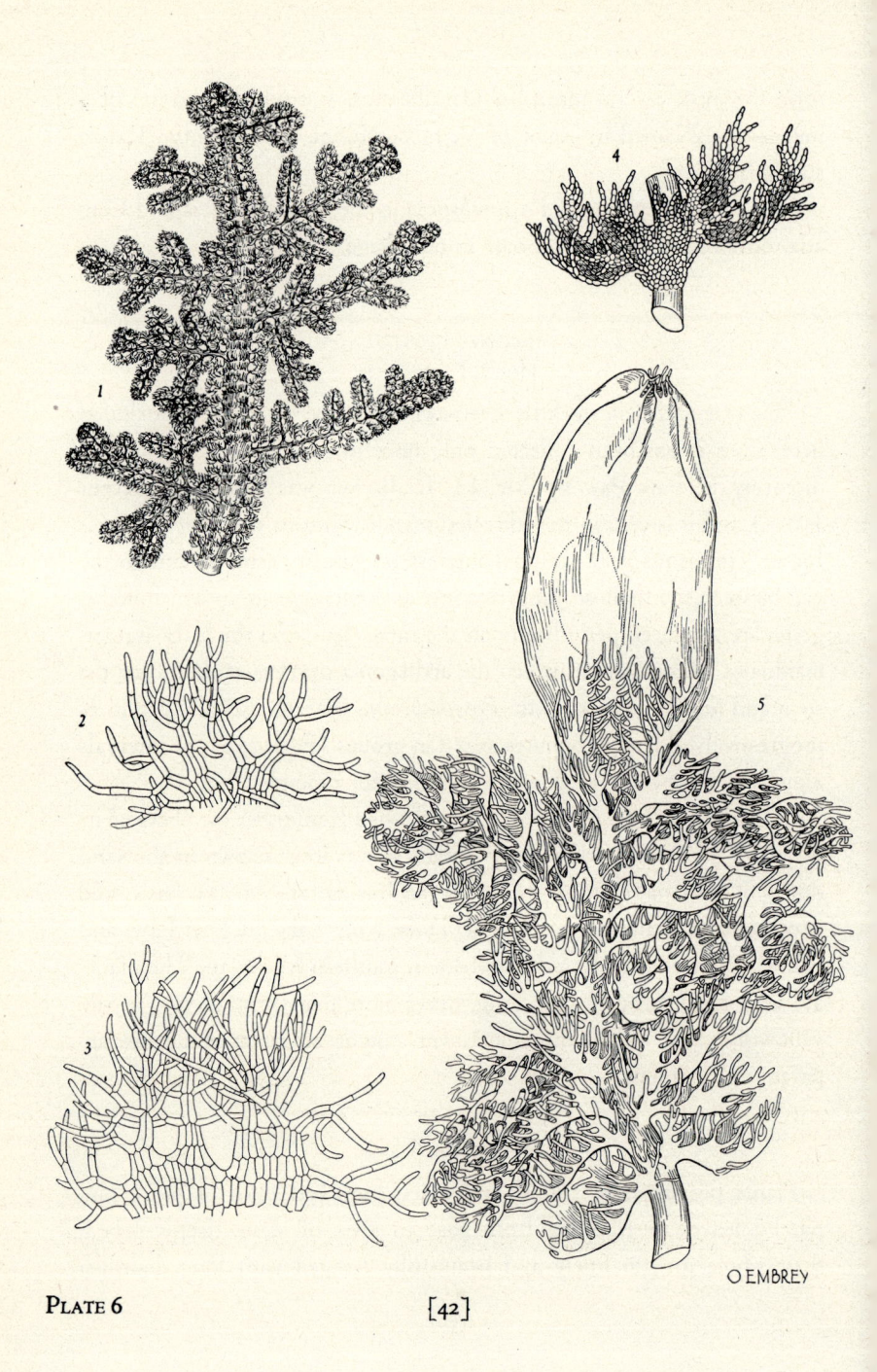

teeth; a third row of leaves, the underleaves, on the lower side of the stem, very much like the other leaves but somewhat smaller. Male plants not different; archegonia and later the sporophyte terminal on the stem or a main branch, in a large, club-shaped perianth, with a contracted, fringed mouth; capsule subglobose. Named from the Greek *ptilidion,* a little feather, from the much divided leaves.

Three species occur in North America, of which one is known in our range.

PTILIDIUM PULCHERRIMUM (Web.) Hampe
Plate 6, Figures 4, 5

This is a very common liverwort in Michigan, especially in the northern part, yet is often passed by and not seen because of its reddish- to golden-brown coloration which matches too well its substratum. It grows most commonly on bark at the base of trees and shrubs in swamps and woods, much more rarely on boulders. The thin, tough mats tear away from the substratum very easily and remain in one piece. When the large, club-shaped perianths (Fig. 5) are produced at all, they usually occur in large numbers and serve to make the plants much more conspicuous. Although hard to see in the field, this is one of the most beautiful plants under the lens, especially a compound microscope, because of the complex fringing and clear color which help make field identifications easy.

Ptilidium ciliare (L.) Hampe, a very common species in northern Michigan, especially in the Upper Peninsula, may eventually be discovered in our range. It differs from *Ptilidium pulcherrimum* in its larger size and in the erect stems which grow in tufts 2-4 cm. deep. Furthermore, it grows on sandy soil or rocks, not on wood.

EXPLANATION OF PLATE 6
Figs. 1-3, Trichocolea tomentella: 1, branch X4, 2, underleaf and 3, leaf X40; Figs. 4-5, Ptilidium pulcherrimum X15: 4, detail of leaves and underleaf, 5, branch with perianth.

Trichocolea Dumort.

Plants large, soft, pale grayish-green, 1-3 times pinnately branched; leaves deeply lobed nearly to the base, each segment in turn divided into numerous simple or branched threads so fine that the succubous leaf arrangement is obscured; underleaves resembling the leaves, but much smaller. Archegonia at the end of the stem or a main branch, without a perianth, the developing sporophyte protected by a combination of the much enlarged archegonium and a fleshy outgrowth of the stem; capsule oblong, very rarely produced. Name from the Greek *thrix, trichos,* hair, and *coleos,* sheath, from the fleshy calyptra which bears numerous finely divided leaf-like structures.

Although a large number of species have been described from the tropics, only one occurs in the United States and Canada.

Trichocolea tomentella (Ehrh.) Dumort.
Plate 6, Figures 1-3

This is one of our handsomest and most conspicuous leafy liverworts. It grows most luxuriantly on the ground in deep, wet, arbor vitae swamps, but as such habitats are rare in southern Michigan, the species is correspondingly uncommon with us. Once found, however, it will not be easily forgotten, because of the large size of the plants, which may reach 10 or 15 cm. in length, and the pale, grayish-green color. The large, pinnately branched plants somewhat resemble some mosses, especially the feather moss *(Hypnum)* and the fern moss *(Thuidium)*. Under a lens, however, the fine, thread-like divisions of the leaves (Fig. 3) make *Trichocolea* quite unmistakeable. Under a microscope, the capillary branches resemble the filaments of some alga.

Blepharostoma Dumort.

Plants very small, clear to yellowish-green; branches lateral, irregular in arrangement; leaves attached almost transversely, divided very nearly to the base into usually 4 (rarely 3 or 5) lobes of one thickness of cells throughout; underleaves exactly as the leaves, but slightly smaller and often consisting of fewer lobes. Antheridia terminal on branches; archegonia terminal on the stem or branches; perianth cylindrical at the base, triangular in the upper part, the mouth contracted, fringed with hair-like teeth; capsule oval. Name from the Greek *blepharon*, lash, and *stoma*, mouth, from the hair-fringed mouth of the perianth.

Of two species in North America north of Mexico, one occurs in Michigan.

BLEPHAROSTOMA TRICHOPHYLLUM (L.) Dumort
Plate 7, Figures 1-4

In our range this liverwort creeps around among other liverworts and among mosses, instead of growing in large, pure patches. Because of its scattered manner of growth and its small size, it is most apt to be found completely by accident during the examination of some other species collected on rotten wood. In northern Michigan, however, it grows in large mats on rotten logs, more rarely on rocks. The delicate plants, hardly 10 mm. long, with their leaves divided to the base into parallel, hair-like teeth, are not likely to be confused with any other species in our region. If question does arise, a microscopic examination will settle it at once, for in this liverwort the lobes of the leaves consist of only one row of cells (Figs. 3, 4) and are never more than one cell wide or thick. *Trichocolea* is very much larger, and does not usually grow on rotten wood and almost never on rocks.

LEPIDOZIA (Dumort.) Dumort.

Plants in rather pale green mats, regularly pinnately or bipinnately branching, some of the branches tapering to a thread-like tip with much smaller leaves; leaves overlapping from the base toward the apex of the stem, each one divided half its length or more into usually 4 finger-like lobes; underleaves almost exactly like the leaves, differing only in smaller size and occasionally having one less lobe. Antheridia

PLATE 7 [46]

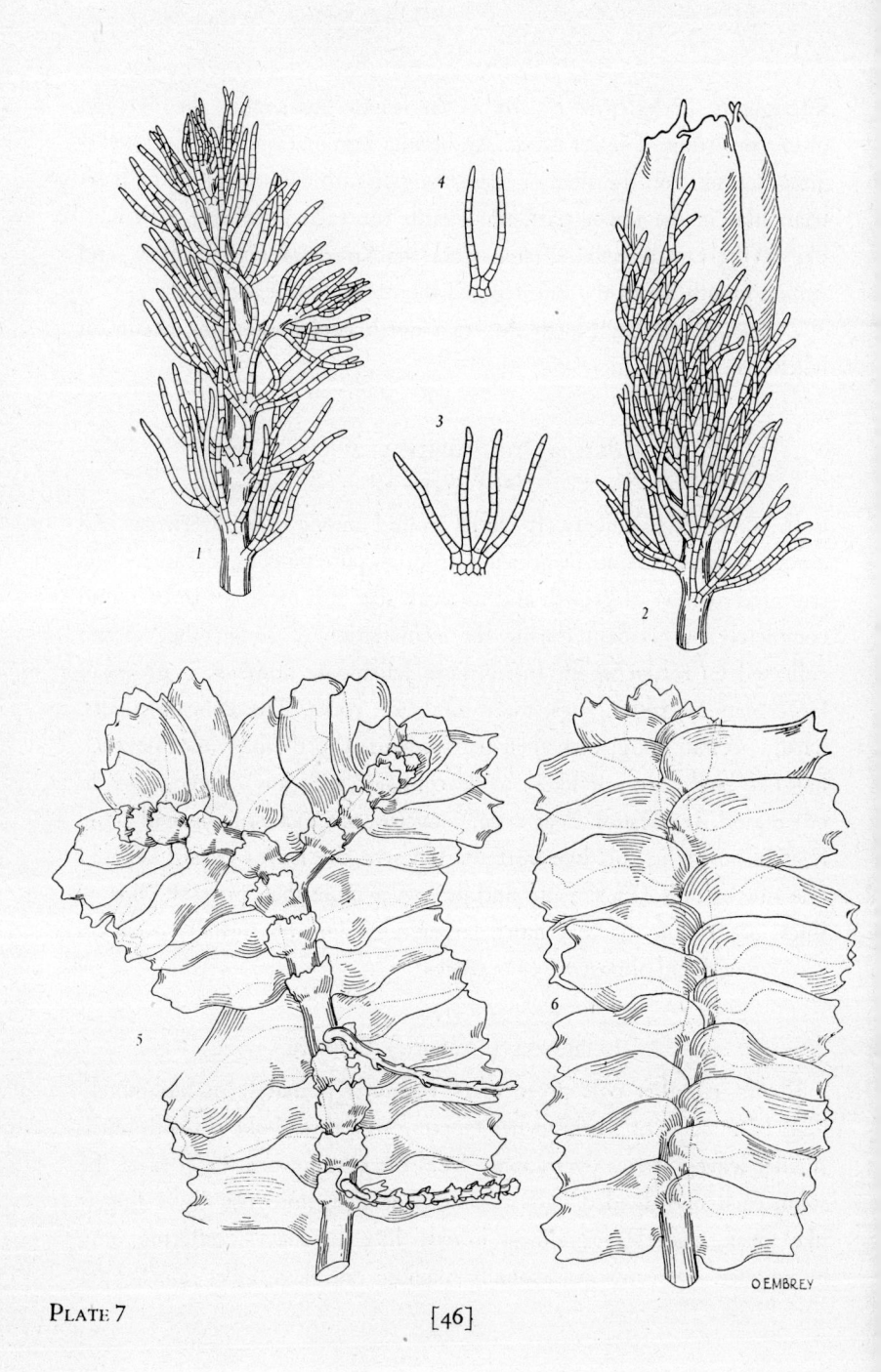

and archegonia on short ventral branches; perianth spindle-shaped, triangular in cross section near the mouth, which is usually somewhat toothed. Name from Greek, *lepis,* scale, and *ozos,* branch, from the form of the leaves surrounding the perianth.

Of six species in temperate North America, only one is known to occur in southern Michigan.

LEPIDOZIA REPTANS (L.) Dumort.
Plate 8, Figures 1-4

The grayish- or bluish-green color of this hepatic, and its regular pinnate branching, serve as excellent characters for field identification. Closer examination will reveal the characteristic tapering branches, and especially the 4-lobed leaves bent downward like small, thumbless hands. This liverwort is not particularly common in southern Michigan, but becomes much more common northward. It grows in moist places, either as separate plants among mosses and other liverworts, or in thin, flat mats on rotten wood or rich humus. *Lepidozia reptans* is an unusually distinct liverwort and will not be easily confused with any other liverwort. Even the other species of *Lepidozia* which occur in northern Michigan are very different in their much narrower leaf lobes and their habit of growing in bogs among peat mosses (*Sphagnum*).

BAZZANIA S. F. Gray

Plants large, olive green or with a brownish tinge; stems erect or prostrate, clearly dichotomously branched, producing from the under side threadlike branches bearing small leaves; leaves overlapping from base to apex of the stem, nearly flat, narrowed to a three-toothed apex; underleaves much smaller and of a different shape than the other leaves, roundish, usually 4-toothed or lobed, broader than the

---

EXPLANATION OF PLATE 7

Figs. 1-4, Blepharostoma trichophyllum X40: 1-2, sterile and fruiting plants, 3, leaf and 4, underleaf; Figs. 5-6, Bazzania trilobata X10: lower and upper side of stem.

PLATE 8 [48]

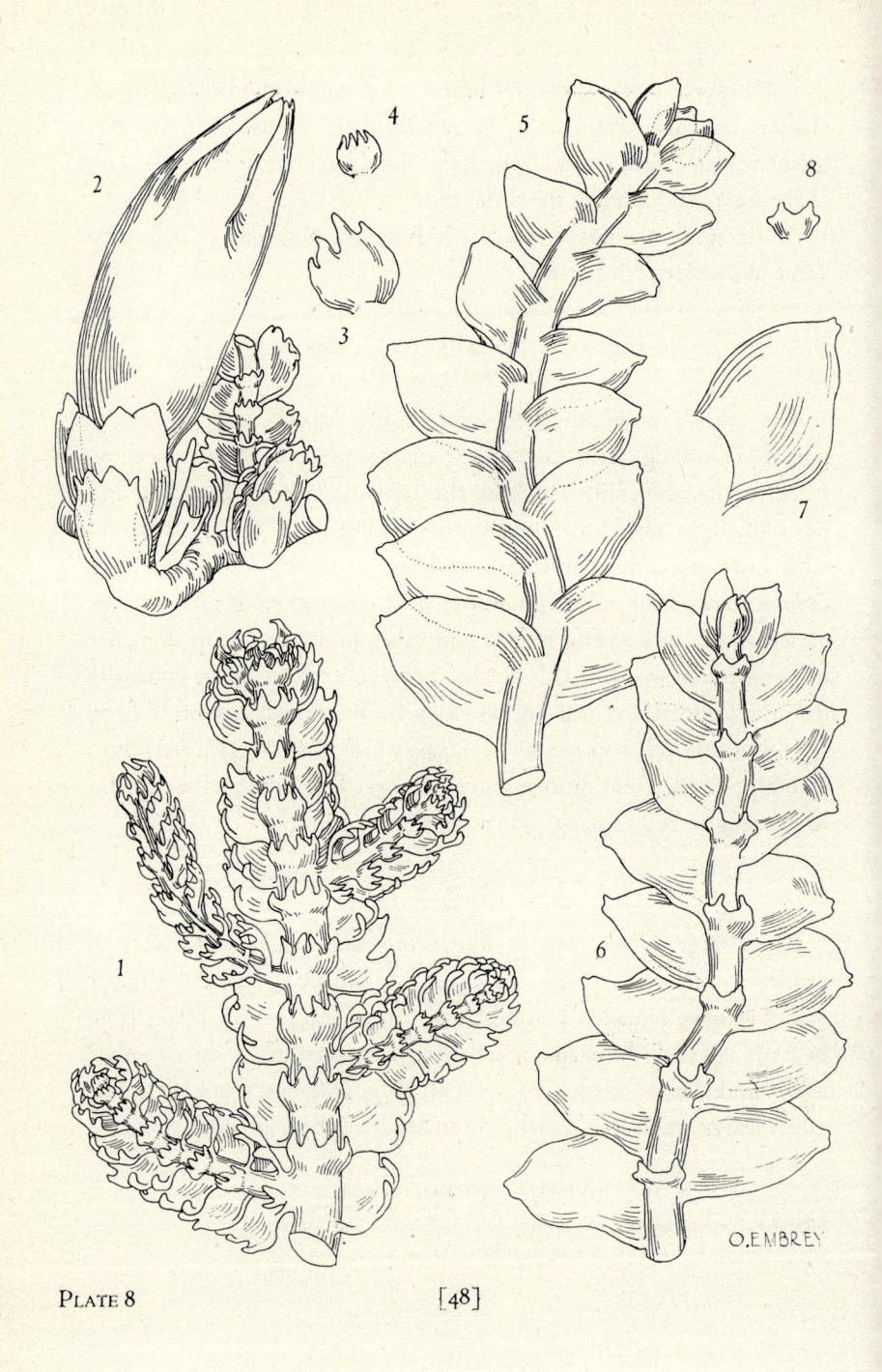

stem. Antheridia and archegonia on short ventral branches; sporophytes extremely rare in our range, in spindle-shaped perianths obscurely triangular in section, fleshy at the base; capsule oblong. Named originally "Bazzanius" by S. F. Gray, in honor of some friend.

Six species of *Bazzania* are known in temperate North America, and many more in the tropics, yet only one occurs in our range.

Bazzania trilobata (L.) S. F. Gray
Plate 7, Figures 5, 6

In southern Michigan, this large liverwort occurs almost exclusively on either old stumps or rotting logs, whereas in the Upper Peninsula, it is not uncommon on rock, either on boulders or ledges. In any habitat it produces extensive, rather thick, dark or olive green mats which allow recognition at a distance by their characteristic appearance. The leafy stems reach 5 mm. in width and 10 cm. in length. The asymmetrical leaves with their curious hump near the base of the upper side, and the nearly equal three teeth at the tip distinguish this liverwort from all others.

Calypogeia Raddi

Plants in wide, thin, whitish- or bluish-green mats; stems sparsely and irregularly branching; leaves overlapping from the apex toward the base of the stem, nearly flat, ovate, rounded at the apex, very rarely shallowly notched or indented, the margins without teeth; underleaves always present, up to one-half the size of the leaves, from nearly circular to kidney shaped, usually notched at the apex or deeply divided. Antheridia and archegonia on very short ventral branches; perianth absent; sporophyte developing in a fleshy, tubular, subterranean perigynium to which the calyptra is united nearly its whole length; cap-

---

EXPLANATION OF PLATE 8

Figs. 1-4, Lepidozia reptans X25: 1-2, sterile and fruiting branches, 3, single leaf and 4, underleaf; Figs. 5-8, Calypogeia fissa X25: 5-6, upper and lower sides of stem, 7, single leaf and 8, underleaf.

O. EMBREY

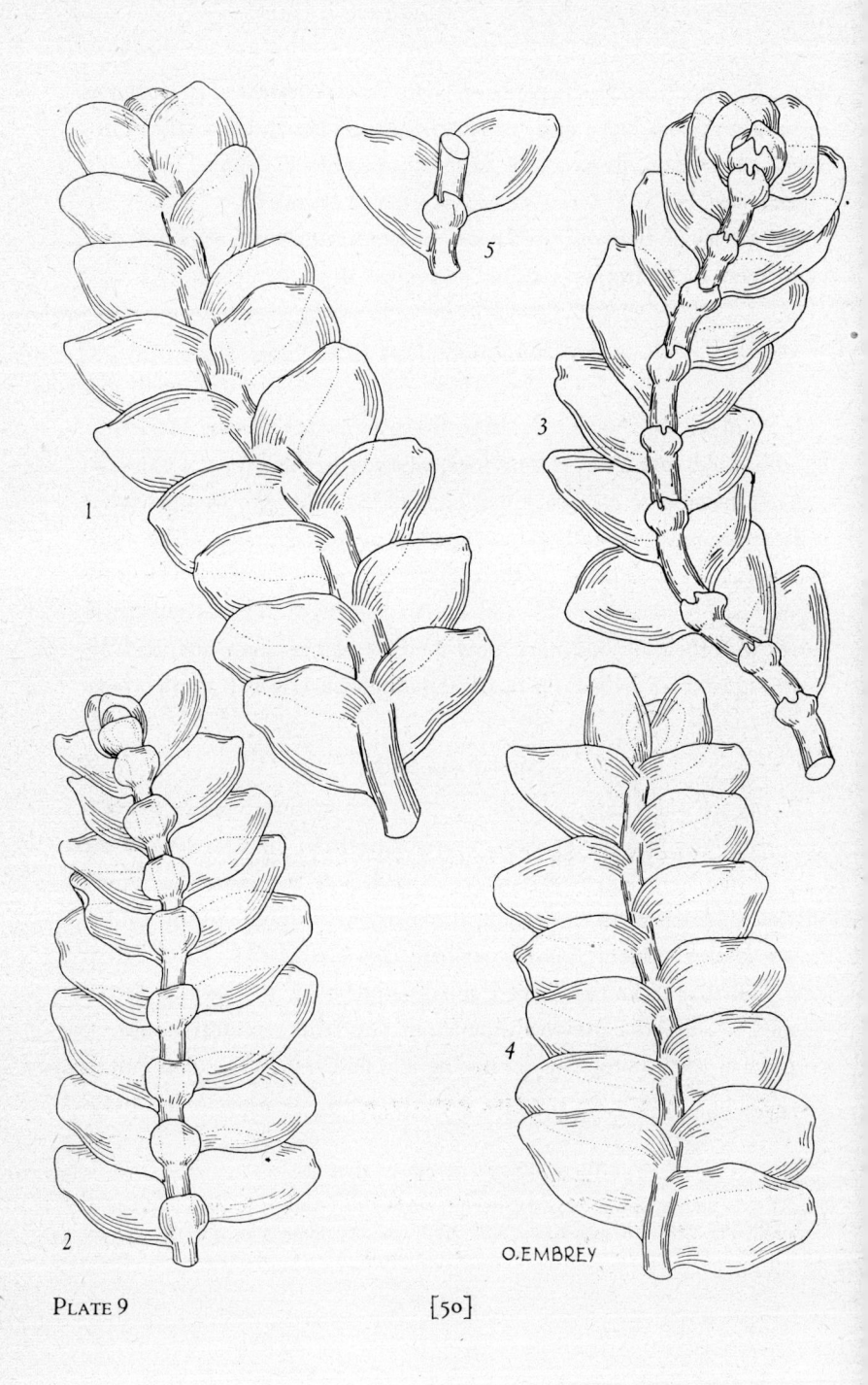

PLATE 9 [50]

sule cylindrical, the four valves by which it opens spirally twisted. Name from Latin *calyx,* cup, and *hypogaeus,* underground, from the subterranean perigynium.

Seven species of *Calypogeia* are known from temperate North America, of which the following are not uncommon in southern Michigan.

Key to the species of *Calypogeia*

1. Underleaves not or very shallowly and obtusely notched (Pl. 9, fig. 2) ....*Calypogeia Neesiana*

   Underleaves divided at least one-quarter of their length 2

2. Each lobe of the underleaf bearing a supplementary tooth at one side; many of the leaves notched or indented at the apex (Pl. 8, figs. 6, 8) ....*Calypogeia fissa*

   Underleaf without lateral teeth; leaves commonly not notched at the apex (Pl. 9, figs. 3, 5) ....*Calypogeia Trichomanis*

CALYPOGEIA TRICHOMANIS (L.) Corda
Plate 9, Figures 3-5

On shaded, moist soil, whether clay on a wooded hillside, or humus in a swamp, will be found this whitish- or bluish-green, nearly transparent liverwort. The plants lie prostrate on the ground, although the tip of the stem may suddenly become erect and bear a spherical cluster of pale gemmae. The flat, ovate leaves, the somewhat heart-shaped underleaves, and the head-like clusters of gemmae all aid in the recognition of this very characteristic liverwort.

CALYPOGEIA NEESIANA (Massal. et Carest.) K. Müll.
Plate 9, Figures 1, 2

Although this species is very commonly mistaken for the preceding one, it is easily distinguished by the much more shallowly notched or

EXPLANATION OF PLATE 9

Figs. 1-2, Calypogeia Neesiana X15: upper and lower sides of stem; Figs. 3-5, Calypogeia Trichomanis X15: 3-4, lower and upper sides of stem, 5, detail of lower side of stem.

PLATE 10 [52]

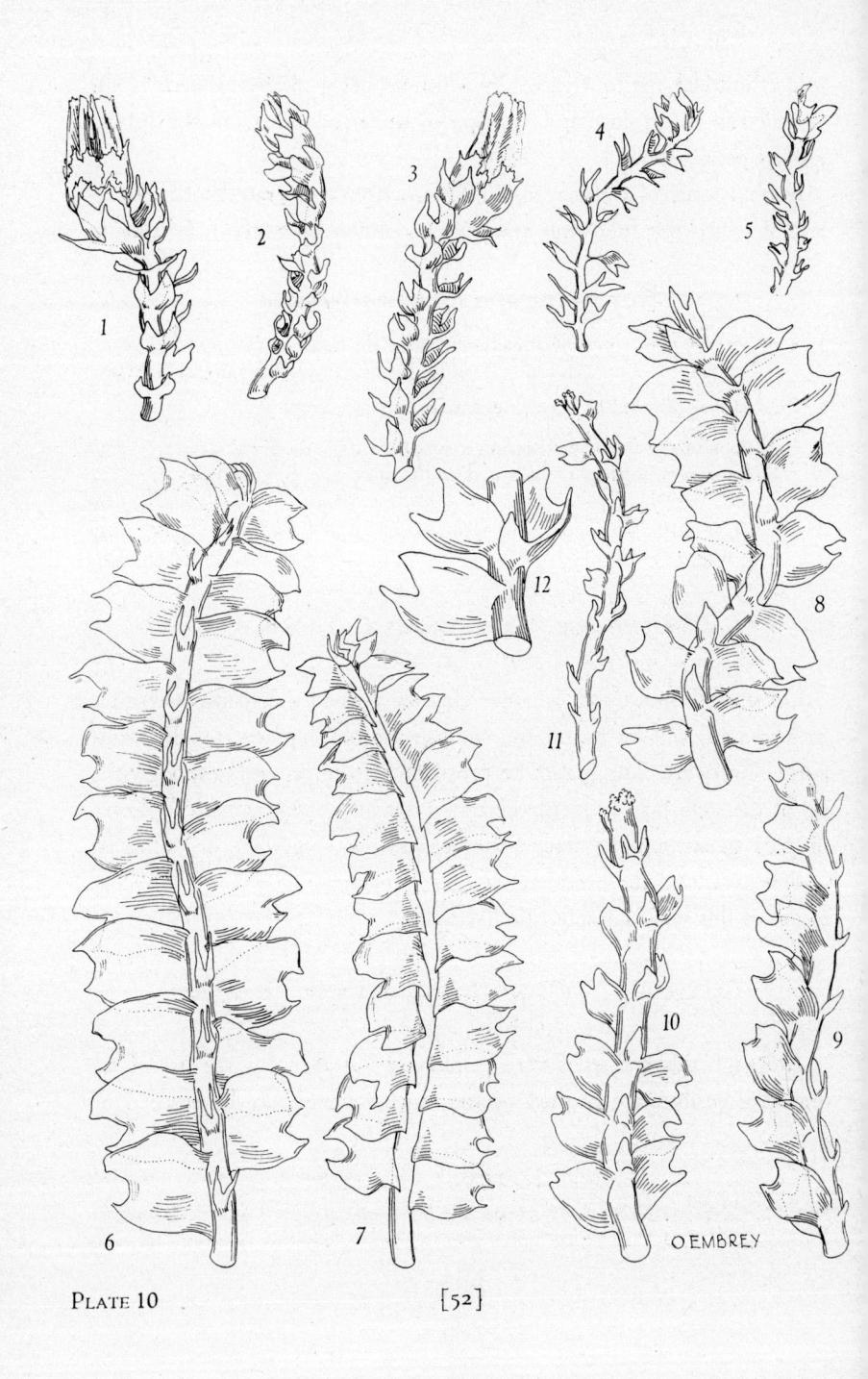

indented underleaves. Also, it grows more frequently on rotten wood and humus than on clay or sandy banks. It is the most common species of *Calypogeia* in northern Michigan, but is somewhat rare in our area.

CALYPOGEIA FISSA (L.) Raddi
Plate 8, Figures 5-8

This liverwort is apparently widely distributed in Michigan, even though it has not been collected many times. It is known in our area only from near Grand Ledge, where it grows on shaded hillsides among mosses. Nevertheless it is safe to predict that it will turn up elsewhere in southern Michigan. It grows on humus and over mosses, and is usually less closely attached to its substratum than the preceding species, from which it is easily distinguished by the much more deeply notched underleaves with a supplementary tooth at each side, and the notched leaf tips.

HARPANTHUS Nees

Plants small, yellowish-green, irregularly branched; leaves overlapping from base to apex of stem, notched at the tip or shortly 2-lobed; underleaves large, narrowly triangular, rarely with a small tooth at one side, mostly united at its base with the upper edge of the leaf just below. Antheridia and archegonia on very short ventral branches; perianth oblong or ovate, narrowed above, united with the calyptra through most of its length, and of several layers in thickness below. Name from Greek *harpe,* sickle, and *anthos,* flower, from the sharply curved or bent archegonial branch from which the perianth develops.

One species of *Harpanthus* occurs in Michigan, out of the two species known.

EXPLANATION OF PLATE 10
Figs. 1-5, Cephaloziella Hampeana X25: stems, some with perianth; Figs. 6-7, Geocalyx graveolens X15: lower and upper sides of stem; Figs. 8-12, Harpanthus scutatus: 8-11, lower side of stem X25, 12, detail of lower side X40.

HARPANTHUS SCUTATUS (Web. et Mohr) Spruce
Plate 10, Figures 8-12

This small liverwort grows in pale or yellowish-green patches on rotting logs which have lost their bark. Although it has been collected in Michigan only in a few places, it is probably fairly common, but overlooked because of its small size. In a swampy woods in southern Oakland County, nearly every fallen log was covered with a dense growth of *Harpanthus,* to the exclusion of other liverworts. The sharply notched or bilobed leaves probably cause this species to be passed over as a small or underdeveloped form of *Lophocolea* or *Chiloscyphus.* The triangular, undivided underleaf, united at its base to the leaf just below it, is absolutely unmistakeable, however, and will serve to distinguish *Harpanthus* from liverworts superficially resembling it.

GEOCALYX Nees

Plants in thin, wide, dark or dull green mats, which often have a curious greasy or oily appearance; branching irregularly; leaves overlapping from the base toward the apex of the stem, sharply and evenly notched; underleaves conspicuous, divided nearly to the base into two equal parts which are not at all toothed at the side. Antheridia and archegonia are on short ventral branches, the archegonial branch becoming, as the sporophyte develops, a fleshy, pendulous, subterranean perigynium united in large part to the calyptra; perianth absent; capsule oval-cylindric. Name from Greek *gae,* earth, and *calyx,* cup, from the subterranean development of the sporophyte-containing perigynium.

The single known species of *Geocalyx* is very common in our range.

GEOCALYX GRAVEOLENS (Schrad.) Nees
Plate 10, Figures 6, 7

On the roots of trees, rotten wood, moist soil, or even on shaded rocks, will be found this common liverwort. The bilobed leaves resemble those of *Lophocolea* and *Chiloscyphus,* but the notching is much sharper and more regular than in either of the others. Furthermore, *Geocalyx* has a curious dull green, often greasy, tinge which contrasts very strongly with the pale or yellowish-green color of *Lophocolea* and the non-aquatic species of *Chiloscyphus*. The unique features of *Geocalyx*, which enable it to be identified without question, are the subterranean perigynium, the complete lack of a perianth, and the underleaves without teeth at the sides.

CHILOSCYPHUS Corda

Plants in pale to dark green mats; stems branched irregularly, not at all pinnate; leaves overlapping from base to apex of stem, their attachment almost parallel to the axis of the stem, roundish to oblong, not notched, or somewhat bilobed, always without marginal teeth; underleaves always present, deeply divided into two lobes, each lobe usually with a lateral tooth. Antheridia produced along the main stem or on long branches, protected by an inrolled lobe at the base of the upper side of a leaf; archegonia on a very short lateral branch; perianth short, bell-shaped, with a broad, 3-lobed mouth, beyond which the large calyptra usually extends; capsule oval. Name from Greek *cheilos,* mouth, and *scyphos,* calyx, from the occasionally two-lipped appearance of the perianth and calyptra after the capsule has burst through them.

Of the five species of *Chiloscyphus* in temperate North America, three are not uncommon in Michigan.

Key to the species of *Chiloscyphus*

1. Leaves indented to sharply bilobed at the apex; plants very pale green, usually growing on rotten wood (Pl. 12, figs. 1-3)..................*Chiloscyphus pallescens*
   Leaves entire, not notched or indented at the apex; plants clear to dark green, growing in wet places... 2
2. Plants very dark green to almost black, attached to submerged stones and sticks in running water (Pl. 11, figs. 1, 2)..................*Chiloscyphus rivularis*
   Plants dull green, growing in very wet bogs and swamps, but not in running water (Pl. 11, figs. 3, 4)..................*Chiloscyphus fragilis*

O.EMBREY

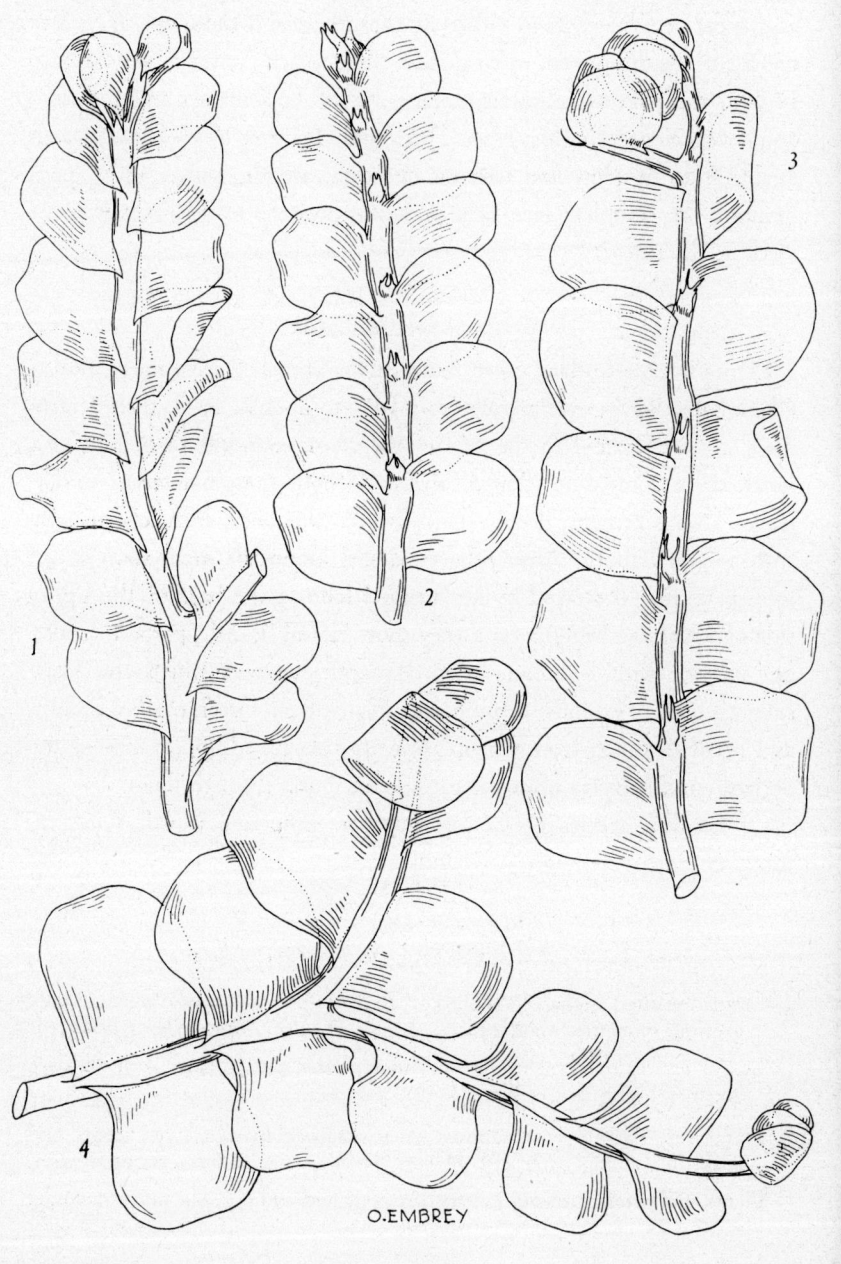

PLATE 11 [56]

CHILOSCYPHUS PALLESCENS (Ehrh.) Dumort.
Plate 12, Figures 1-3

This is one of the commonest liverworts in southern Michigan, where it grows on old logs, both with and without bark, on moist soil (but never in water) and rarely on shaded rocks. From the pale green color, the only slightly notched or bilobed leaves and the deeply divided underleaves with a small tooth at each side, it resembles *Lophocolea heterophylla*. However, it may be definitely distinguished by the different position of the perianth in the two liverworts. In *Chiloscyphus* the archegonial branch is so short that the perianth and sporophyte seem to be produced from the side of the main stem, whereas in *Lophocolea* the perianth and sporophyte are at the very end of the stem or of a long branch. In the absence of perianths, some of the leaves of *Chiloscyphus* will almost certainly show the characteristic folds or sacs which cover the antheridia (Pl. 11, fig. 2). The other species of *Chiloscyphus* need not be confused with this one because of their very different habitats.

CHILOSCYPHUS RIVULARIS (Schrad.) Loeske
Plate 11, Figures 1, 2

Very few liverworts are truly aquatic, although most of them prefer rather moist situations. Consequently, this species is easy to identify, through its habit of clinging to stones, roots or branches in running water, especially in brooks through cedar swamps. Its very dark green color, also, is strikingly different from the pale yellowish-green of the preceding species. Further, the stems are much branched and the leaves are scarcely or not at all indented or notched at the apex. In our range this species is very rare, but becomes more common northward.

EXPLANATION OF PLATE 11

Figs. 1-2, Chiloscyphus rivularis X10: upper and lower sides; Figs. 3-4, Chiloscyphus fragilis X10: lower and upper sides of stem.

CHILOSCYPHUS FRAGILIS (Roth) Schiffn.
Plate 11, Figures 3, 4

On the ground and over rotten logs in very wet places, although rarely actually in the water, grows this species, which is one of the largest leafy liverworts in the state. The stems may become 4-5 cm. long and 4-5 mm. broad. The leaves range from almost circular to somewhat squarish, but are never either notched or bilobed. In addition to its large size, *Chiloscyphus fragilis* is distinguished by its habit from *Chiloscyphus pallescens,* which prefers much drier situations, and from *Chiloscyphus rivularis,* which grows in running water. Also, *Chiloscyphus fragilis* is more or less intermediate in color between the other two.

LOPHOCOLEA Dumort.

Plants whitish- or yellowish-green, soft and creeping; stems branching irregularly; leaves overlapping from base to apex of stem, attached nearly parallel to the axis of the stem, deeply notched and therefore bilobed, or truncate; underleaves always present, deeply divided into two lobes, each of which bears a tooth at the side. Antheridia and archegonia terminal on the main stem or a long branch; perianth usually oblong, sharply triangular in cross section, the angles often winged or keeled, not at all united to the calyptra. Name from Greek *lophos,* crest, and *coleos,* sheath, from the coarsely toothed, winged perianth.

Of eight species of *Lophocolea* in the United States and Canada, two are known in Michigan.

Key to the species of *Lophocolea*

1. Leaves regularly bilobed, covered with dusty, yellowish-green gemmae (Pl. 12, figs. 7, 8) ....*Lophocolea minor*

   Leaves entire, indented, or sharply bilobed, all types on the same stem; gemmae usually lacking (Pl. 12, figs. 4, 5) ....*Lophocolea heterophylla*

LOPHOCOLEA HETEROPHYLLA (Schrad.) Dumort.
Plate 12, Figures 4-6

This is probably the commonest and most widely distributed leafy liverwort in Michigan. It occurs as pale green mats on rotten logs, at the base of trees, on moist soil both in the open and under trees, and even on shaded rocks. When invading new areas, it produces circular colonies, of which the outermost (and newest, of course) branches have very small, deeply and sharply notched leaves. Older plants in the same colony show the characteristically dissimilar leaves, some bilobed, some shallowly notched or indented, some truncate, and some rounded, which are responsible for the specific name. Perianths are ordinarily produced in profusion on older plants, and their position at the end of the stem and main branches clearly separates this liverwort from *Geocalyx graveolens*, which has no perianth at all, and from *Chiloscyphus pallescens*, in which the perianth is on an exceedingly short lateral branch from the main stem. In cross section the perianth is distinctly an equilateral triangle, of which one flat side is ventral and one angle is dorsal. It is to be distinguished from *Geocalyx*, also, by the supplementary teeth on the underleaves, and by the paler color and more translucent appearance. It differs from the following species in the almost complete lack of gemmae.

LOPHOCOLEA MINOR Nees
Plate 12, Figures 7, 8

The status of this species has been the source of much argument, and many authors have considered it to be only a variety of the preceding species. In Michigan, however, the two liverworts are so distinct and so easily distinguishable, even in the field, that I do not hesitate in keeping them separate. *Lophocolea minor* grows in much drier places than *Lophocolea heterophylla*, is smaller, paler colored, and has the unique characteristic of producing special reproductive bodies or gemmae on the margins of the leaves. By the end of the growing season the leaves have been almost completely eroded away by the transformation of the vege-

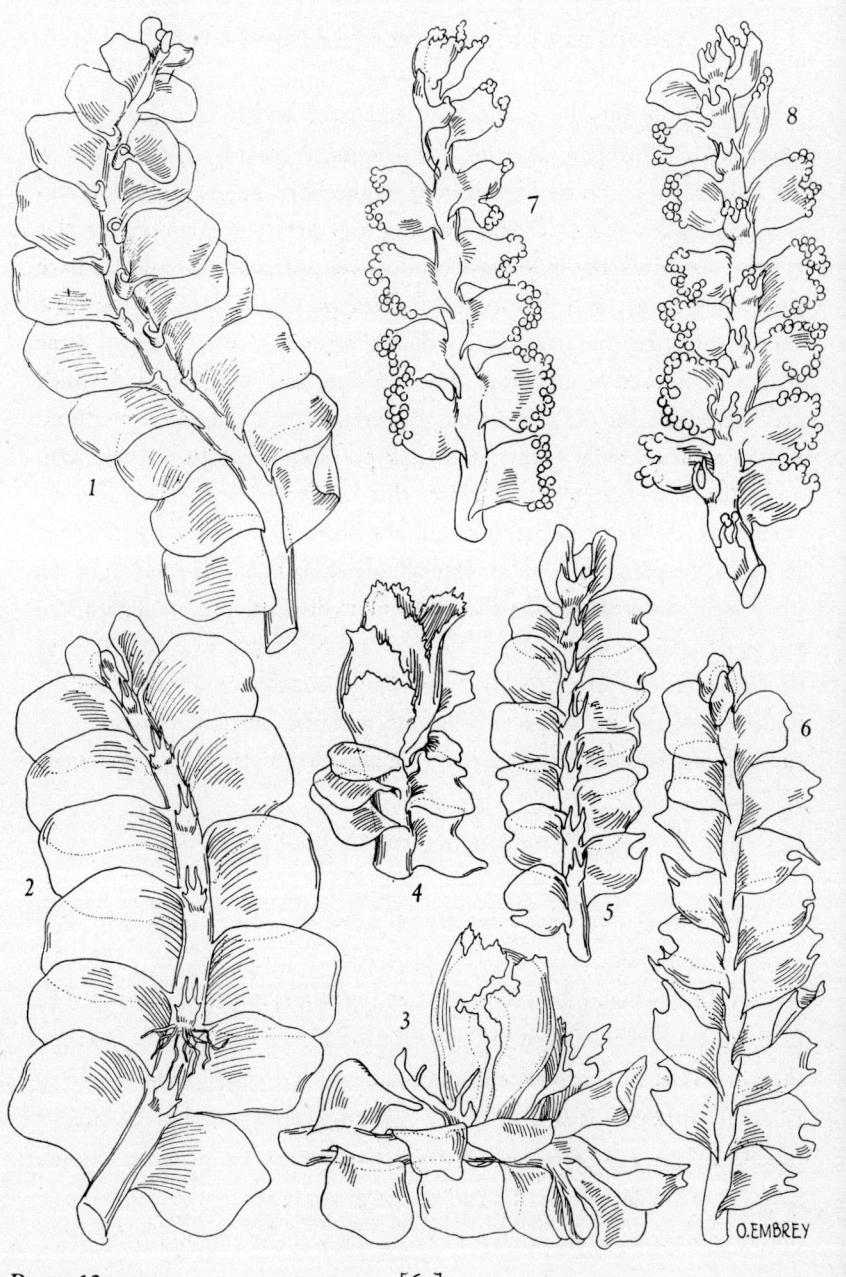

PLATE 12 [60]

tative cells into countless gemmae. The concentration of the small, spherical gemmae (Figs. 7, 8) at the leaf margins gives the whole plant, and the mat of plants, which is already yellowish-green, a curious dusty appearance. This species is especially common on shaded clay or sand banks in the woods or along lakes and streams; much more rarely on rotten wood or at the base of trees. The production of very small gemmae in great numbers is the unique feature of *Lophocolea minor* and serves in southern Michigan to distinguish it from all other liverworts with sharply two-lobed leaves.

CEPHALOZIELLA (Spruce) Schiffn.
Plate 10, Figures 1-5

Plants extremely small, the smallest of liverworts, reddish- or brownish-green; stems short, little branched; leaves narrow, not or only slightly wider than the stem, attached at right angles to the stem, deeply divided by a sharp apical notch into two entire or toothed lobes; underleaves small or absent. Antheridia on the main stem or a branch; archegonia at the end of the main stem or of a long branch, the leaves of archegonial stems larger than on sterile stems; perianth pear-shaped or rectangular, triangular to hexagonal-prismatic in cross section, never with long teeth at the mouth. Gemmae are produced at the stem apex in many species, and are of importance in identification, but require the use of a microscope. Name a diminutive of *Cephalozia* (which see).

Twenty-seven species of *Cephaloziella* are recognized in North America north of Mexico.

The species of *Cephaloziella* grow on soil, either among mosses or other liverworts, or in tufts on otherwise unoccupied and often surprisingly dry and exposed earth and rock. The plants are so small that, although common and widely distributed, they are almost universally

EXPLANATION OF PLATE 12

Figs. 1-3, Chiloscyphus pallescens X15: 1-2, upper and lower sides of stem, 3, stem with perianth; Figs. 4-6, Lophocolea heterophylla X15: 4, young perianth, 5-6, lower and upper sides of sterile stem; Figs. 7-8, Lophocolea minor X25: upper and lower sides of sterile stem.

PLATE 13   [62]

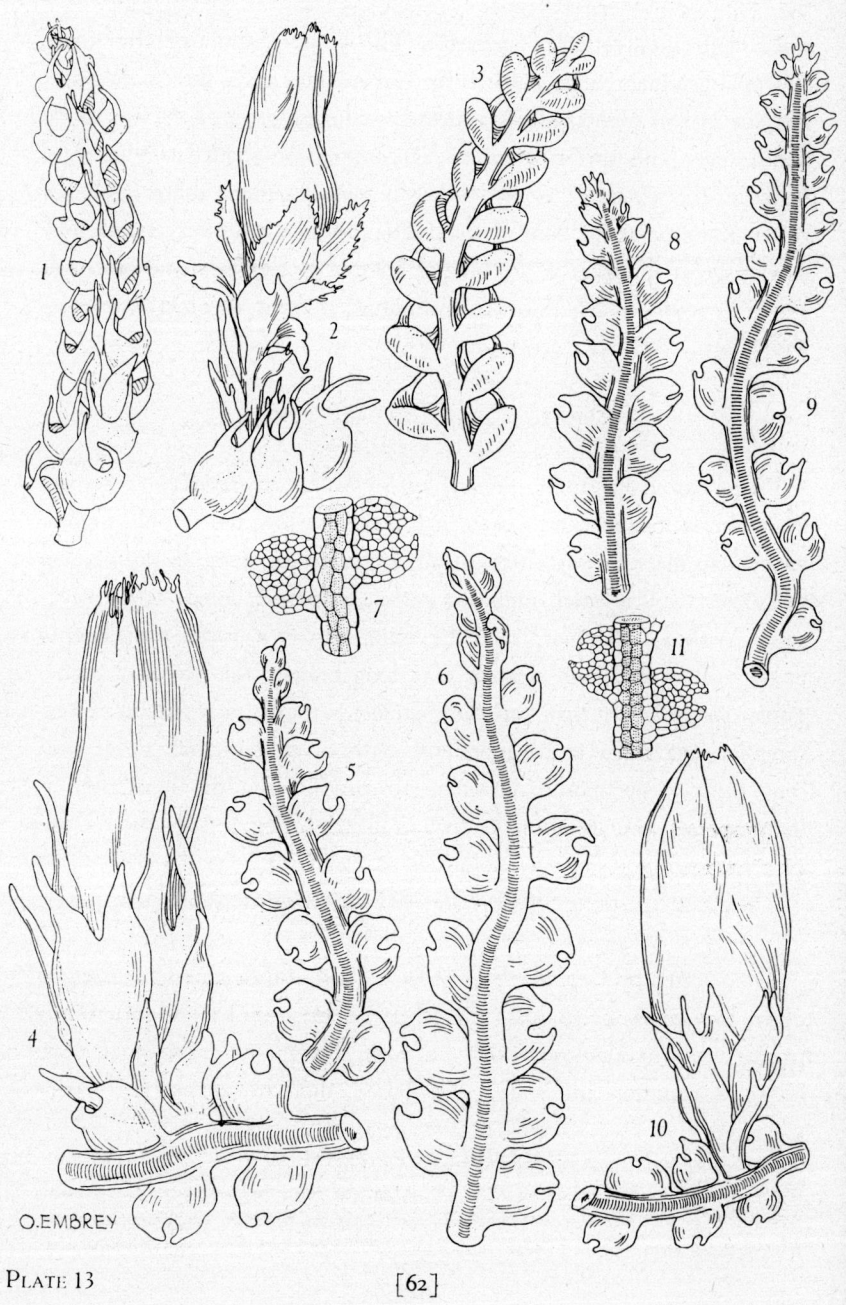

overlooked. Furthermore, their identification requires careful examination of specimens under a compound microscope. Because of the difficulties in distinguishing between the half dozen species which occur in Michigan, a discussion of them is beyond the scope of this work. The commonest species in our range seems to be *Cephaloziella Hampeana* (Figs. 1-5), which, together with several other species, is characterized by its entire leaves and possession of antheridia and archegonia on the same plant.

CEPHALOZIA Dumort.

Plants very small, in pale or bluish-green mats; stems unbranched or with a few branches from the lower side, made up of very large, transparent cells; leaves overlapping from the base toward the apex of the stem, attached obliquely to the stem, concave, with two acute to acuminate lobes separated by an acute or rounded apical notch; underleaves completely lacking. Antheridia and archegonia on special, short branches; perianth oval to cylindric, clearly three-angled, with the third angle ventral and a flat side dorsal, the mouth shallowly or deeply toothed. Name from the Greek *cephale,* head, and *ozos,* branch, from the swollen, head-like cluster of archegonia and leaves which surround them at the end of a short branch.

Thirteen species of *Cephalozia* occur in temperate North America, and several of them are known in our range. At least four species may be distinguished by patient study, although this genus of liverworts is not recommended to the beginner as an easy one, since for exact identifications, it is necessary to measure the size of the leaf cells under a compound microscope.

EXPLANATION OF PLATE 13

Figs. 1-3, Nowellia curvifolia X25: 1, 3, upper and lower sides of stem, 2, stem with perianth; Figs. 4-7, Cephalozia connivens X25: 4, detail of perianth, 5-6, lower and upper sides of stem, 7, detail of stem; Figs. 8-11, Cephalozia media X25: 8-9, lower and upper sides of stem, 10, perianth, 11, detail of stem.

Key to the species of *Cephalozia*

1. Leaves as broad as long, nearly circular in outline; divided about one-third their length, the lobes obtuse to acute, directed toward each other, but not meeting 2

   Leaves clearly longer than broad, divided to about one-half, the lobes long pointed, directed toward each other, and actually crossing in some leaves (Pl. 14, figs. 1-4) .... *Cephalozia Loitlesbergeri*

2. Thread-like branches with much reduced leaves (flagella) arising from the lower side of stem; lower edge of leaf not continued down the stem as a wing (decurrent) (Pl. 14, figs. 5-9) .... *Cephalozia pleniceps*

   Flagella absent; leaves strongly decurrent 3

3. Plants usually very dark green; mouth of perianth only faintly toothed, not at all fringed (Pl. 13, figs. 8-11) .... *Cephalozia media*

   Plants usually pale green, mouth of perianth fringed with long, hair-like teeth (Pl. 13, figs. 4-7) .... *Cephalozia connivens*

CEPHALOZIA MEDIA Lindb.
Plate 13, Figures 8-11

This is perhaps the commonest and most widely distributed species of *Cephalozia* in the state. It grows on the ground or among peat mosses in swamps and bogs, as well as on moist earth banks, and may be recognized by the clear, dark green color, the lack of leafless ventral branches or flagella, the separation of antheridia and archegonia on different plants, and the hardly toothed mouth of the perianth.

CEPHALOZIA CONNIVENS (Dicks.) Spruce
Plate 13, Figures 4-7

This little liverwort grows on all sorts of substrata, but most commonly on moist soil, humus, or rotten wood, often among mosses, especially peat moss or *Sphagnum*. Its usually pale green color and the presence of antheridia and archegonia on the same plant separate it from *Cephalozia media*. From *Cephalozia pleniceps* it is distinguished by the strongly decurrent leaves and lack of flagella. It differs from both species in the long-fringed mouth of the perianth.

Cephalozia pleniceps (Aust.) Lindb.
Plate 14, Figures 5-9

Although common enough in northern Michigan, this species is rather rare in our region, where it grows on rotten wood and humus in bogs and swamps. It is to be separated from the two preceding species by its characteristic small, thread-like, leafless branches or flagella, from the lower side of the stem. The flagellate branches anchor the stems to the substratum or to other plants so efficiently that they are too easily broken off when the stems are pulled off for examination, and so are apt to be missed. The lower margin of the leaf does not extend down the stem as a wing, as in *Cephalozia connivens*, but is clearly and distinctly cut off from the stem. Further, the mouth of the perianth is scalloped or somewhat toothed, but not fringed with long teeth.

Cephalozia Loitlesbergeri Schiffn.
Plate 14, Figures 1-4

In the northern part of our range, on and among plants of the peat moss, *Sphagnum*, grows a very small, pale *Cephalozia* without flagella. The leaves, instead of being nearly circular as in the preceding three species, are longer than wide. The lobes are directed toward each other and so long that in many leaves they actually cross each other. The mouth of the perianth is long fringed, in contrast to that of *Cephalozia. media* and *Cephalozia pleniceps*. In addition to the different leaf shape, it is distinguished from *Cephalozia connivens*, which also has a fringed perianth mouth, by the much smaller leaf cells.

Nowellia Mitten

Plants green, but usually with a reddish or purplish tinge, in thin mats on rotten wood; stems 1-2 cm. long, less than 1 mm. wide, branching sparingly and irregularly; leaves bent toward the upper side of the stem, attached to the stem almost at right angles by a very narrow base, very concave, deeply bilobed, each lobe with a curved, long, hair-like tip, the

PLATE 14 [66]

lobe toward the lower side of the stem much larger, with a sac-like swelling; underleaves lacking. Antheridia and archegonia at the end of special, short branches; perianth large, swollen-cylindric, conspicuously three-angled toward the broad mouth, which bears long, spine-like teeth. Name in honor of John Nowell, a Yorkshire botanist.

Only one species of *Nowellia* is known, which is widespread through the Northern Hemisphere.

Nowellia curvifolia (Dicks.) Mitten
(*Cephalozia curvifolia* Dumort.)
Plate 13, Figures 1-3

This beautiful little liverwort, which grows almost exclusively on rotten wood, either on fallen trees which have lost their bark, or on stumps, is not uncommon in Michigan. It is readily identified, even when sterile, by the reddish color and the remarkable leaves, which bear long, curved, hair-points and sac-like swellings (Fig. 3). The function of the sacs has been the subject of much discussion, but is still unsettled. Once it has been identified, this species will afterward be recognized at sight.

Cladopodiella Buch

Plants closely resembling *Cephalozia* in appearance, forming large, dark green to brownish-red mats or tufts; stems sparingly branched, except for the numerous, thread-like, leafless ventral branches or flagella; the outer layer of cells not large and transparent as in *Cephalozia;* leaves notched only one-fifth or one-fourth their length, at most, the lobes blunt; underleaves not only present but often conspicuous. Antheridia on the end of a short branch or on the main stem; archegonia

EXPLANATION OF PLATE 14

Figs. 1-4, Cephalozia Loitlesbergeri X15: 1, perianth, 2-3, upper and lower side of stem, 4, detail of cell arrangement; Figs. 5-9, Cephalozia pleniceps X15: 5-6, lower and upper sides of stem, 7, perianth, 8-9, detail of cell arrangement; Figs. 10-13, Cladopodiella fluitans X15: 11, 13, upper side of stem, 10, 12, lower side of stem.

on short ventral branches; perianth short cylindric, lobed at the mouth but not at all toothed. Name a diminutive of *Cladopus* (in which, as a subgenus of *Cephalozia,* the two species were long retained), from the Greek *clados,* a branch, and *pos,* foot or stalk, from the sporophyte at the end of a short ventral branch.

Of two species known, one occurs commonly in northern Michigan, and only just reaches the area under consideration here.

Cladopodiella fluitans (Nees) Buch
(Cephalozia fluitans Spruce*)*
Plate 14, Figures 10-13

As already pointed out under *Chiloscyphus rivularis,* aquatic leafy liverworts are so unusual that, when found, they are not at all difficult to identify. This liverwort grows most commonly in pools of standing water in peat bogs, and in addition to the unusual habitat, it may be recognized by the shallowly notched leaves with blunt lobes, the presence of underleaves, and the abundant ventral flagellate branches.

Odontoschisma Dumort.

Plants in green or brownish mats, stems 1-5 cm. long, nearly all the branches from the lower side of the stem; ventral flagella present; leaves overlapping from base to apex of stem, attached obliquely or almost parallel to the axis of the stem, almost circular, without teeth of any sort, not or scarcely notched; underleaves present, small to conspicuous. Antheridia and archegonia on short ventral branches; perianth large, pleated and 3-angled, contracted toward the mouth, which is toothed; capsule oval. Name from the Greek *odous, odontos,* tooth, and *schisma,* splitting, from the commonly deeply split perianth.

Of the six species of *Odontoschisma* in North America north of Mexico, only one is known in our range.

Odontoschisma denudatum (Mart.) Dumort.
Plate 18, Figures 3-5

This liverwort grows in green or brownish mats on rotten logs and humus in swampy woods. The leaves usually become smaller toward the tip of the stem, which bears conspicuous clusters of very small yellow gemmae. The underleaves are not large and can usually be found easily only near the growing tip of the stem. It may be necessary even to examine several plants before underleaves can be demonstrated. The effort is worthwhile, however, as in our range there are very few round-leaved leafy liverworts without infolded lobules which have underleaves and which produce gemmae. It is distinctly a liverwort of moist places and may even be innundated during part of the year. It has been found only once in Oakland County, but then it occurred in a deep, swampy woods on rich humus which had been under water earlier in the spring. *Jamesoniella autumnalis,* with which it is most likely to be confused, differs in the total lack of underleaves and a preference for drier habitats, such as shaded stones, fallen logs, and the base of trees.

Jamesoniella (Spruce) Steph.

Plants in wide, green to golden brown mats over humus, rotten wood and shaded stones; stems prostrate or ascending, irregularly branching; leaves overlapping from apex toward the base of the stem, from nearly circular to oval, rarely very slightly indented at the apex, all leaves convex, without teeth, except those just below the perianth; underleaves absent or rarely present. Antheridia and archegonia at the tip of the main stem and long branches; perianth broadly cylindric, puckered to a narrower, strongly fringed mouth. Name in honor of William Jameson, an English botanist.

Of two American species, one is known in Michigan, where it is common.

PLATE 15 [70]

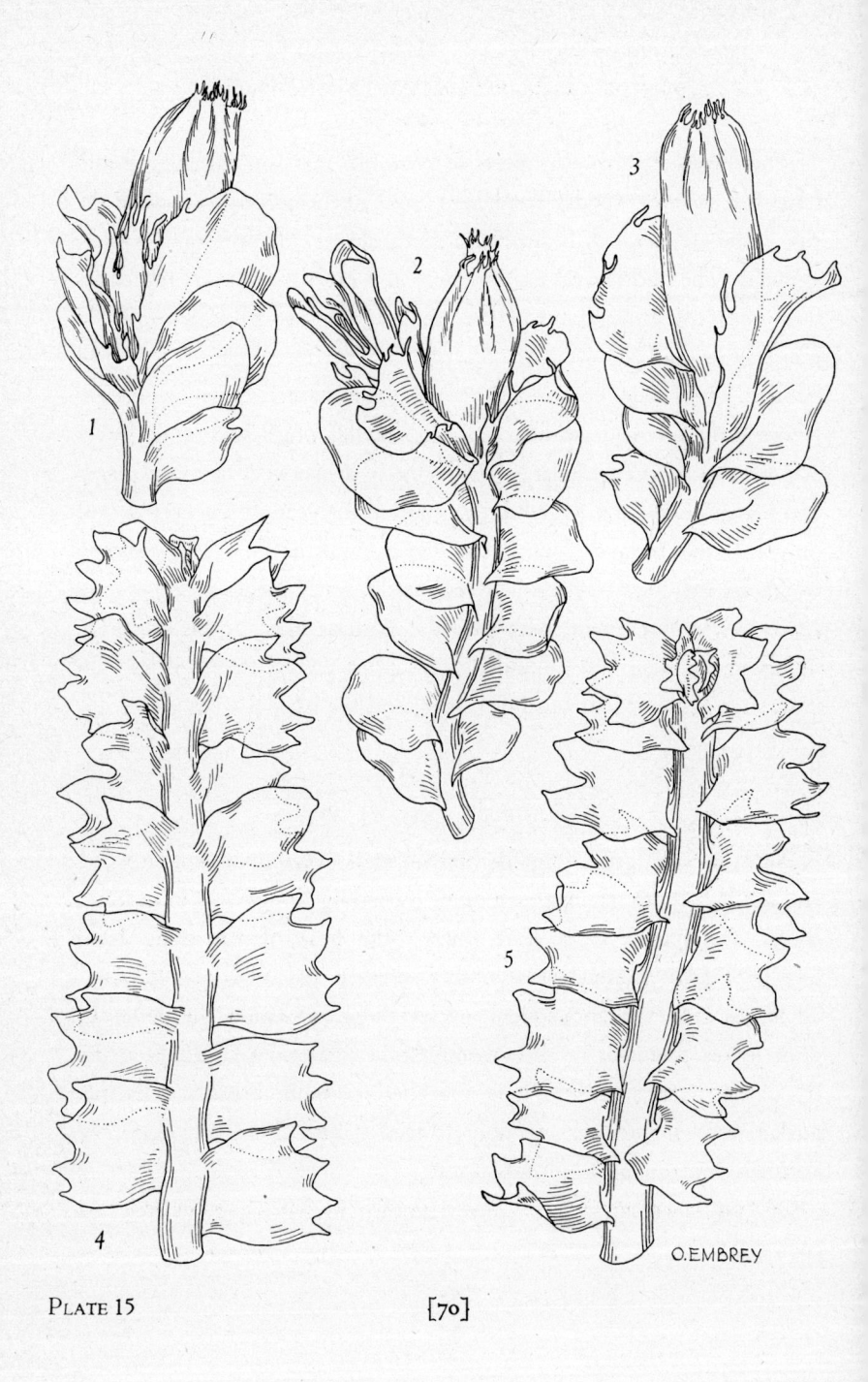

JAMESONIELLA AUTUMNALIS (DC.) Steph.
Plate 15, Figures 1-3

This common liverwort grows in wide mats over rotten logs, at the base of trees, and on shaded stones. Because of the almost circular leaves, it is apt to be confused with several other species, especially *Odontoschisma denudatum* and *Jungermannia lanceolata*. It differs from both, however, in its preference for drier habitats, and especially in the deeply and conspicuously fringed mouth of the perianth. Also, the leaves just below the perianth are usually fringed on the lower edge, and fringed underleaves are sometimes present. These characters can be made out easily with a hand-lens, but will not need to be used long, as after a little experience, the species may be recognized at sight by its characteristic "look." Sterile specimens of *Jungermannia lanceolata* may be recognized by the oblong, not circular, leaves, and of *Odontoschisma denudatum* by the presence of underleaves.

BARBILOPHOZIA Loeske

Plants large, in wide, dark green to reddish-brown mats; stems branching dichotomously, leaves overlapping from apex toward the base of the stem, square to rhombic, divided one- to two-thirds of their length into 3 or 4 acute lobes which are bristle-pointed in some species; underleaves lacking in some species, large and deeply two-parted and fringed in others. Antheridia at the end or at the middle of a main stem; archegonia at the end of a main stem or branch; perianth ovate or pear-shaped, pleated and contracted toward the lobed mouth, which is generally also toothed or fringed. Name from Latin *barbatus,* bearded, and *Lophozia,* a genus name, from the hair-pointed leaf lobes of some species. All three American species occur in northern Michigan, but only the following species has been found in our area.

EXPLANATION OF PLATE 15

Figs. 1-3, Jamesoniella autumnalis X15: 1, lower side and 2-3, upper side of stem, all with perianth; Figs. 4-5, Barbilophozia barbata X15: lower and upper side of stem.

It is certain that some member of the closely related genus *Lophozia* will turn up eventually in our region, since about ten species have been collected in northern Michigan.

BARBILOPHOZIA BARBATA (Schmid.) Loeske
(*Lophozia barbata* Dumort.)
Plate 15, Figures 4, 5

This is not only one of the largest but also one of the most easily identified liverworts in Michigan. The plants form wide, dark green mats over humus, rotten logs and shaded stones in moist or swampy places. The stems, which are covered on the lower side with white rootlets or rhizoids, may reach 5 cm. in length. The leaves are clearly 4-lobed, a condition found, in the species treated here, only in *Lepidozia*, which is much smaller and also possesses conspicuous underleaves very similar to the other leaves. The underleaves very rarely found on *Barbilophozia barbata* are small and inconspicuous, not at all like the other leaves.

JUNGERMANNIA L.

Plants medium sized to small, light to dark green; stems usually flat on the substratum, matted together, branching only slightly; leaves overlapping from the apex toward the base of the stem; circular, oval, sometimes nearly rectangular, without teeth or lobing of any kind; underleaves completely absent. Antheridia and archegonia at the tip of the main stem or branch; the leaves surrounding the archegonia, and later the perianth, no different from the other leaves; perianth cylindrical and suddenly contracted to a tubular beak, or spindle-shaped and pleated, gradually tapered to a narrow mouth. Named in honor of Jungerman, an early German botanist.

Although 13 species of *Jungermannia* are known in temperate North America, only two occur in our area.

Key to the species of *Jungermannia*

1. Perianth tubular, suddenly contracted to a flat or depressed top with a small beaked mouth in its center; plants growing on soil, humus, or rotten wood (Pl. 16, figs. 3, 4)..*Jungermannia lanceolata*

   Perianth spindle shaped, pleated; plants very small, growing directly on wet rock (Pl. 16, figs. 1, 2)..*Jungermannia pumila*

JUNGERMANNIA LANCEOLATA L.
Plate 16, Figures 3, 4

In our range, this liverwort occurs most commonly on moist, shaded banks in ravines, but in northern Michigan it usually grows on humus or on rotting wood, in swamps and deep woods. It forms wide mats of a characteristic pale green color. The leaves are oval or oblong to rectangular, not almost circular as in *Jamesoniella* and *Odontoschisma*. Nearly always present are the characteristic perianths which are cylindrical or nearly so, flat or depressed at the apex, greatly contracted to a small, tubular, beak-like mouth (Figs. 3, 4). Since none of the other liverworts included here have this sort of a perianth, and since the perianths are produced in abundance, this species is one of the easiest to identify, even by the beginner.

JUNGERMANNIA PUMILA With.
Plate 16, Figures 1, 2

Although this liverwort is widely distributed in Michigan, it is known from comparatively few places. In our range it has been collected only on a dripping cliff of calcareous sandstone in the park at Grand Ledge. The scarcity of rock outcrops in southern Michigan and the small size of this liverwort conspire against the discovery of many localities in our region for either it or the next species. However, large boulders in intermittent brooks in shaded ravines, as well as outcroppings of bed rock, should furnish a suitable habitat, and so should be searched carefully for it. The plants occur in thin, dark green tufts or mats directly on the rock, not on a humus layer overlying the rock. The plants have oval

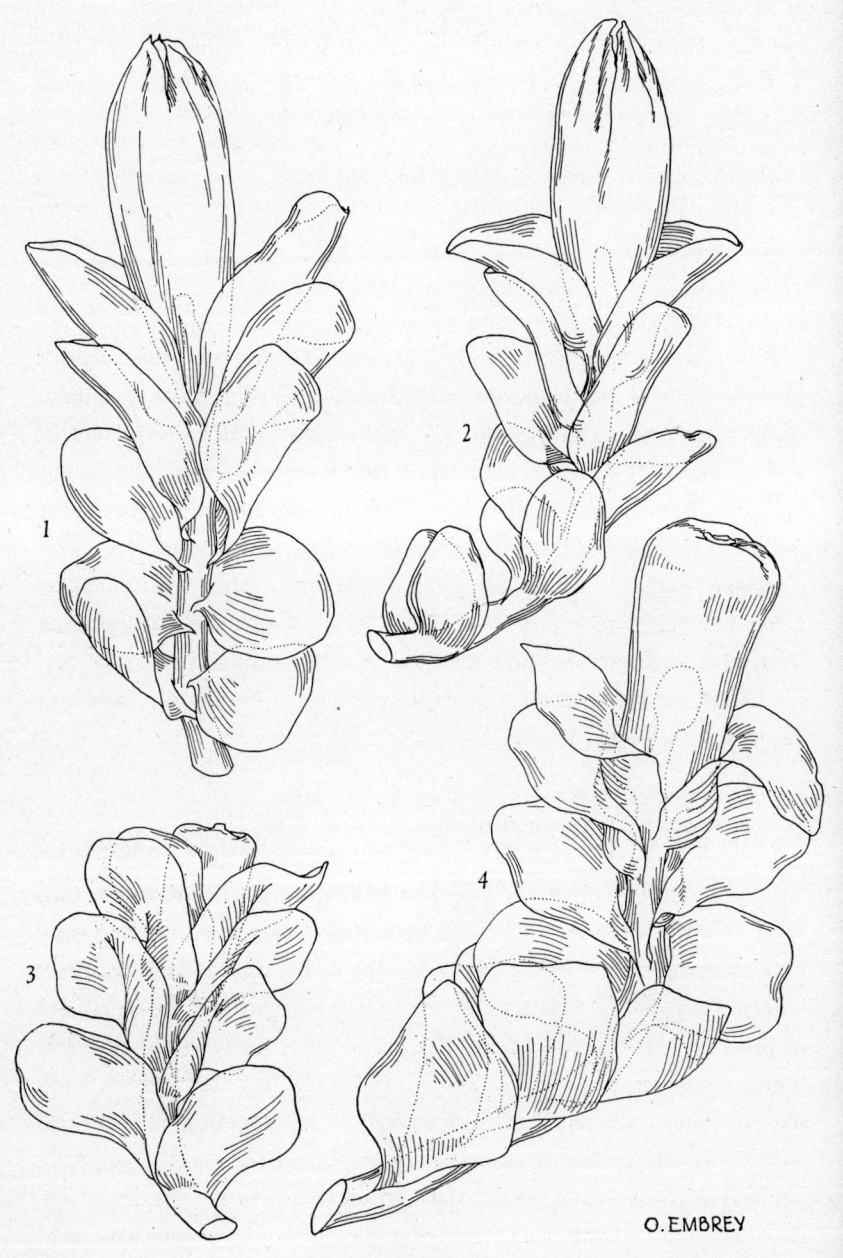

PLATE 16 [74]

leaves, and almost always possess the typically spindle-shaped or bottle-shaped perianth (Figs. 1, 2), which is very different from the cylindrical, beaked perianth of *Jungermannia lanceolata*.

PLECTOCOLEA Mitten

Plants of medium size, much resembling the species of *Jungermannia;* stems slightly branched, from nearly erect to prostrate and matted; leaves overlapping from the apex toward the base of the stem, oval to circular, without teeth or lobes of any sort; underleaves completely absent. Antheridia and archegonia at the end of a main stem or branch, the archegonia and later the perianth surrounded by 2 or 3 leaves which resemble the other leaves but which are united for much of their length with the perianth (Pl. 17, fig. 4), which is egg-shaped or conic. Name from Greek *plectos,* twisted, and *coleos,* sheath, from the twisted apex of the perianth of one species.

Eight species of *Plectocolea* occur in North America north of Mexico, but only one has been recognized in southern Michigan.

PLECTOCOLEA HYALINA (Lyell) Mitten
(Nardia hyalina Carringt.*)*
Plate 17, Figures 1, 4

In northern Michigan this little liverwort is common, and covers square yards of moist sandstone, but in our area it is known only from the interesting ledges and cliffs of calcareous sandstone near Grand Ledge. It grows commonly on soft rock which will hold water, more rarely on compact, moist, sandy soil. The plants are a pale or clear green, usually with some tinge of red. The leaves are very nearly circular, with a broad base attached obliquely to the stem. The leaves of living plants have a very pretty chain-like appearance. Perianths, which are

EXPLANATION OF PLATE 16
Figs. 1-2, Jungermannia pumila X25: upper side of stems with perianth; Figs. 3-4, Jungermannia lanceolata X15: lower and upper sides of stem with perianth.

PLATE 17 [76]

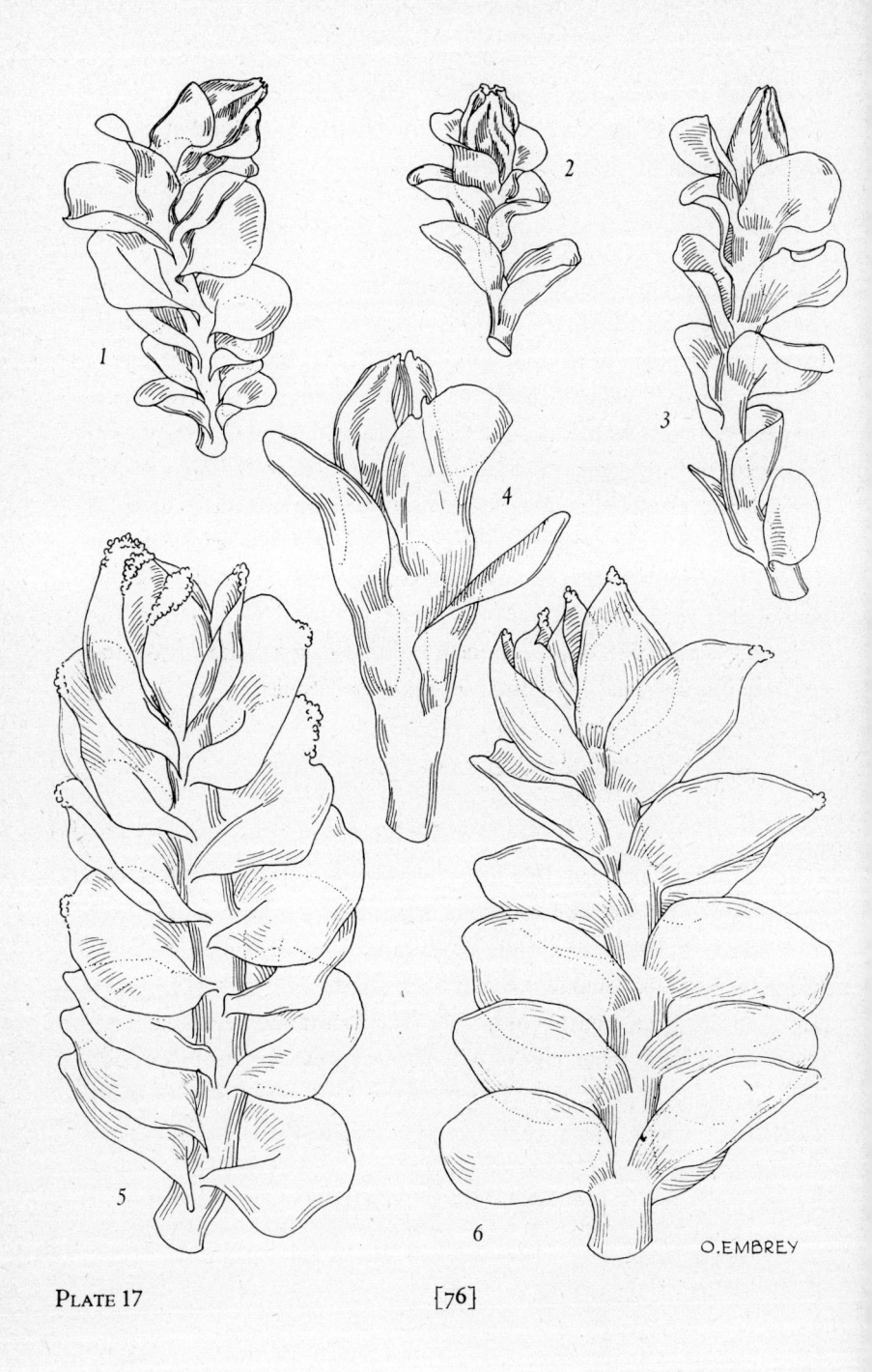

produced rather rarely in our region, provide the most positive means of identification, since only in this genus of our liverworts are the uppermost leaves united to the perianth in a complex, fleshy cup (Fig. 4). The usual habitat of the plants on bare, moist rock is helpful in identifying it, also. It is most apt to be confused with *Jungermannia pumila*, which is smaller, darker green, and has oval, not circular, leaves.

MYLIA S. F. Gray

Plants, with the exception of one species, large, to 10 cm. long, yellowish- or reddish-green, in dense tufts or creeping among mosses; stems unbranched or forking; leaves overlapping from apex toward the base of the stem, oval to nearly circular, their cells very large, visible with a good hand-lens; underleaves present, but so hidden by the rootlets that they may be difficult to demonstrate. Antheridia along the middle of the stem, archegonia at the tip; perianth oblong or oval, flattened toward the wide, two-lipped mouth as though it had been pinched together from the sides. Name originally "Mylius," presumably in honor of some friend of S. F. Gray.

Of three species of *Mylia* in North America, one occurs in Michigan, where it is not uncommon.

MYLIA ANOMALA (Hook.) S. F. Gray
Plate 17, Figures 3-5

One of the most characteristic species of peat-bogs, this liverwort occurs as individual plants creeping through and over *Sphagnum*, the peat moss, or in large, pure tufts. The leaves are nearly circular along the greater length of the stem, but at the growing tips they are much longer than wide, and pointed, their edges covered with pale or dusty

EXPLANATION OF PLATE 17

Figs. 1-4, Plectocolea hyalina: 1, upper side and 2-3, lower side of stem X15, 4, detail of perianth X25; Figs. 5-6, Mylia anomala X15: upper and lower sides of stem, showing gemmiferous leaves.

PLATE 18 [78]

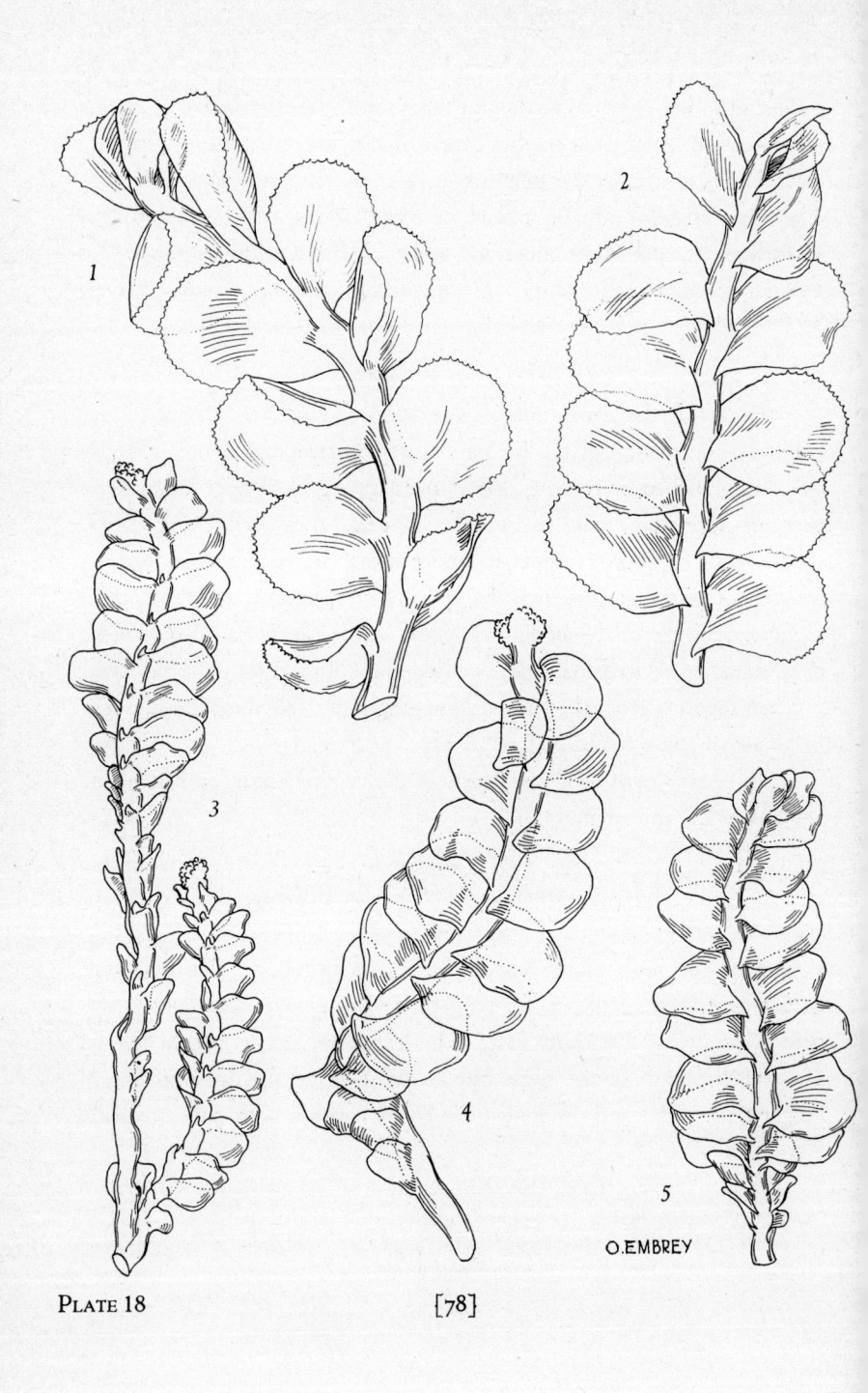

yellowish-green gemmae. This is one of the very few liverworts with circular leaves, which are neither toothed nor lobed, which also has underleaves. Because of the felt-like mass of rhizoids which surround them, the underleaves are usually somewhat difficult to observe with a hand-lens. Nevertheless, even if the underleaves cannot be demonstrated, this species may be identified by its large size (3-5 mm. broad) and the habitat in peat bogs. The large cells, and the pointed upper leaves which bear gemmae are unique features. Our only other liverwort with which it might be confused is *Odontoschisma denudatum,* which is much smaller, with very minute leaf cells, and bearing gemmae not at the margins of pointed leaves, but at the tip of the elongated stem.

PLAGIOCHILA Dumort.

Plants usually large, in extensive, dark green tufts or loose mats; stems to 10 cm. in length, irregularly branched, erect or depressed; leaves overlapping from the apex toward the base of the stem, smaller and farther apart at the base of the stem, oval or circular, nearly always toothed around the margin with sharp teeth, the lower margin nearly straight, folded back under at its attachment to the stem; underleaves normally absent. Antheridia and archegonia at the end of a main stem or branch; the leaves surrounding them usually resembling the other leaves; perianth approximately cylindrical, flattened toward the wide, often 2-lipped, fringed mouth, as though it had been pinched together from each side. Name from Greek *plagios,* oblique, and *cheilos,* mouth, from the 2-lipped perianth which often appears oblique because bent.

There are several hundred species of *Plagiochila* in the world, and 13 in temperate North America, but only one species occurs in Michigan.

EXPLANATION OF PLATE 18

Figs. 1-2, Plagiochila asplenioides X10: lower and upper sides of stem; Figs. 3-5, Odontoschisma denudatum X15: 3, lower side and 4-5, upper side of stem.

PLAGIOCHILA ASPLENIOIDES (L.) Dumort.
Plate 18, Figures 1, 2

Although puzzling forms of this common and conspicuous liverwort will be found, it generally has so characteristic an appearance or "look," that once known it will always be recognized on sight. The plants straggle through other liverworts and mosses as individual stems, or form wide, loose, pure mats, usually on the ground. The stems are not flat on the ground, but are usually erect, especially at the tip. The leaves, when normally developed, are unique in their numerous small, sharp teeth around the margins. No other liverwort of our region has leaves like this one. Unfortunately for the beginner, however, when the habitat is not moist enough or is otherwise unsuited to this liverwort, underdeveloped plants without any marginal teeth on the leaves are the result. The leaves are nevertheless characteristic in the straight lower edge which is folded back underneath, and in the furrow parallel to it. If enough plants are examined, some leaves with normal teeth will always be found.

SCAPANIA Dumort.

Plants large, usually in extensive tufts or mats, leafy stems erect or ascending, arising from a creeping, naked stem flat on the substratum; branches few, irregular; leaves deeply two-lobed, the lobes folded together so that the larger lobe is beneath and the smaller lobe is above, usually sharply toothed or fringed around the margin; underleaves completely lacking. Antheridia and archegonia at the tip of a main stem or branch; perianth oblong, cut off squarely at the wide, often toothed or fringed mouth, not tapering, always strongly flattened as though pinched from top to bottom. Name from Greek *scapanion,* spade, from the flat, spade-shaped perianth.

This very large genus is represented in North America by some 25 species and in Michigan by 11 species, of which only one occurs in our range.

Scapania nemorosa (L.) Dumort.
Plate 19, Figures 1-6

This liverwort is distinctly rare in the area treated here, although very common in northern Michigan. It has been collected only at Grand Ledge, where it grows directly on sandstone ledges and blocks. It is to be distinguished at sight by the curious arrangement of the larger lobe being folded beneath the smaller upper lobe (Figs. 1, 2). The plants are often tinged with red and usually bear masses of dark gemmae among the leaves at the tip of the stem. Under a compound microscope it will be seen that the gemmae consist of a single cell, whereas most other species of *Scapania* have gemmae consisting of two or more cells. The long sharp teeth around the margin of the leaf remind one of *Plagiochila*, whose leaves, of course, are neither lobed nor folded.

Radula Dumort.

Plants of medium size, very pale yellowish-green to brownish-green, in flat mats up to several inches in diameter; stems growing flat on the substratum, somewhat pinnately branching; leaves overlapping from the base toward the tip of the stem, deeply two-lobed, with the smaller, lower lobe or lobule folded in tightly to the upper one, both without teeth of any sort, each lobule bearing a cluster of rootlets from its lower surface; underleaves completely absent. Antheridia and archegonia at the end of the stem; perianth rectangular, spade-like, two-lipped, strongly flattened as though pinched from top and bottom. Gemmae present in some species, circular, flat, produced from the edge of the leaf. Name from Latin *radula,* a scraper, from the perianth, which is shaped like a paint scraper or putty knife.

Twelve species of *Radula* are known to occur in the United States and Canada, but only one of them is recognized in our area.

PLATE 19 [82]

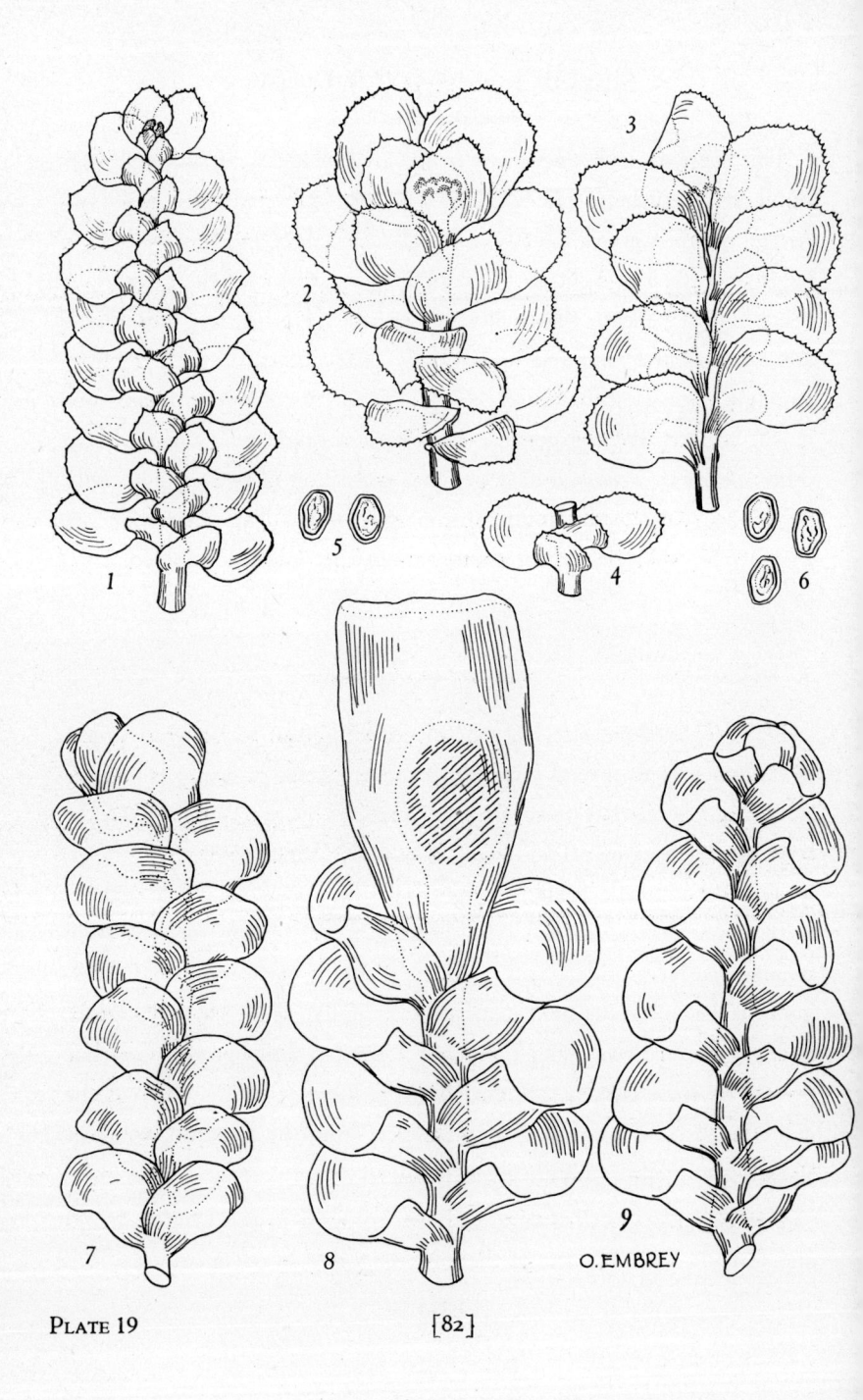

Radula complanata (L.) Dumort.
Plate 19, Figures 7-9

The pale yellowish-green color and habit of growing well up on the trunks of trees, as well as on their base, makes this common liverwort an easy one to recognize at sight. In the arbor vitae swamps of Oakland County, nearly every tree bears one or more of the light colored, circular patches. In deep woods, it occurs on hardwoods and also on shaded rocks. The species of *Frullania,* another genus of liverworts which grow on tree trunks well above the ground, range in color from dark green to reddish-brown. Under a lens or even with the naked eye, the flat, spade-shaped perianths, which are generally produced in great abundance, are evident. The lack of underleaves, the nearly 4-sided lobules, and the circular gemmae produced on the margin of the leaves are unique features which make identification of this liverwort easy.

Porella L.

Plants large, dark to brownish-green; stems usually regularly pinnately branched, leaves overlapping from base to tip of stem, only the pair just below the perianth with teeth of any sort, deeply two-lobed, the lower lobe (lobule) closely folded to the much larger upper lobe, and nearly parallel to the stem; underleaves always present, somewhat wider than the lobules, not divided or notched. Antheridia and archegonia at the end of short side branches; perianth oval, three-angled in section, somewhat flattened toward the toothed, wide, two-lipped mouth. Name a diminutive of the Latin *porus* a passage or pore, probably from the opening of the perianth.

Of nine temperate American species of *Porella,* only one is easily recognized in our region.

EXPLANATION OF PLATE 19

Figs. 1-6, Scapania nemorosa: 1-2, upper and 3, lower side of stem X5, 4, detail of stem X5, 5-6, gemmae X300; Figs. 7-9, Radula complanata X25: 7, upper and 8-9, lower side of stem, 8 with perianth.

PLATE 20 [84]

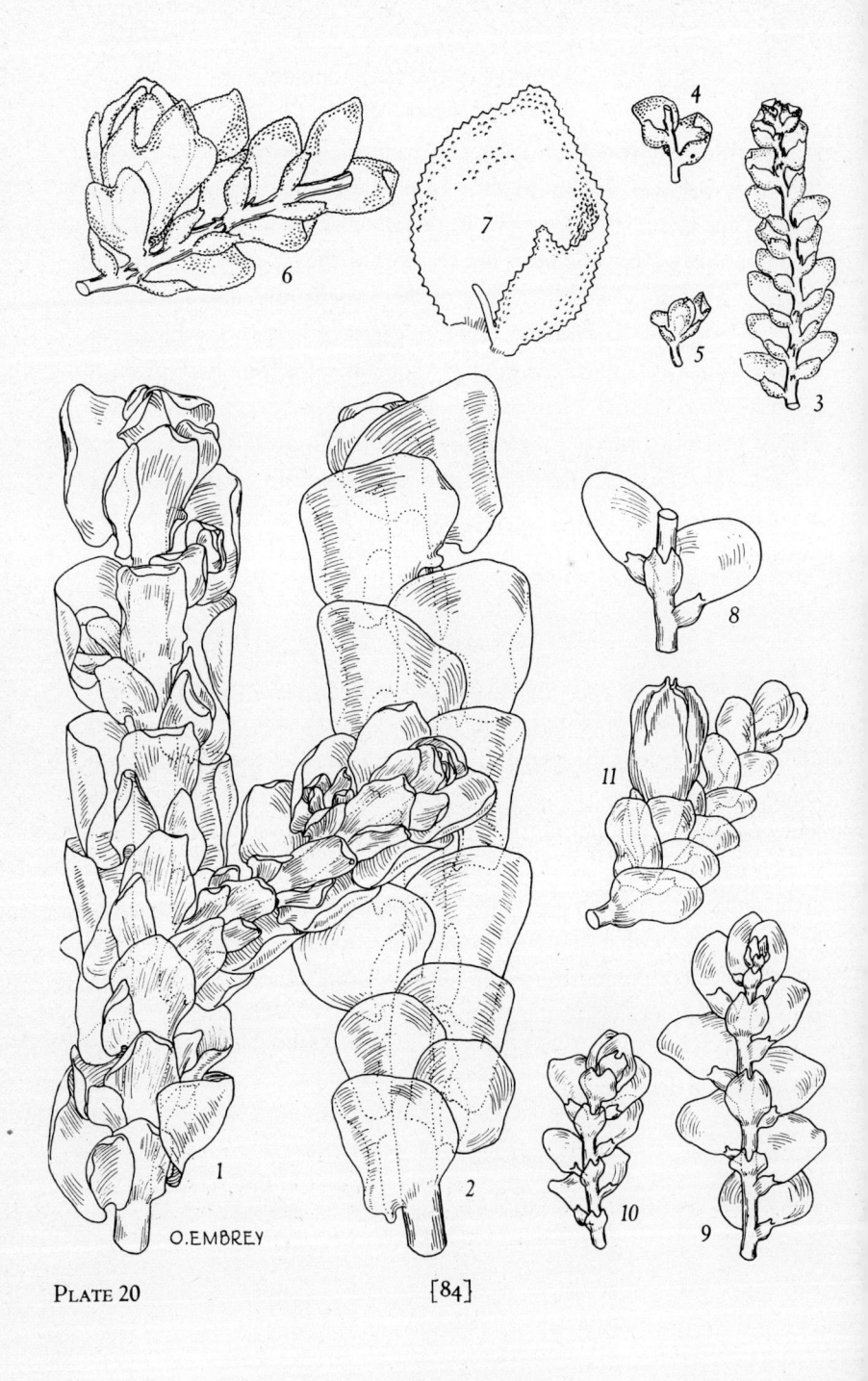

PORELLA PLATYPHYLLOIDEA (Schwein.) Lindb.
Plate 20, Figures 1, 2

Widely distributed in the United States, this plant is common through Michigan. It grows most commonly at the base and over the roots of trees in moist woods, but may occur up on the trunks of trees or on moist soil or shaded rocks. On the base or trunk of trees the stems usually grow in shelf-like expansions. The large, dark or olive green plants, which reach 10 cm. in length, and 4 mm. in width, with both lobules and underleaves, are so characteristic that this liverwort will be as easily recognized on sight as identified in· the first place.

Porella platyphylla (L.) Lindb. is so closely related to *Porella platyphylloidea* that the two species can hardly be separated even by experts. Because of its rarity in Michigan and the difficulty in distinguishing it, *Porella platyphylla* is omitted here.

COLOLEJEUNEA (Spruce) Schiffner

Plants very small, in pale, whitish- or yellowish-green tufts or mats; stems short, 2-8 mm. long; leaves overlapping from base toward the tip of stem, their cells covered with minute spines in most species, rounded or pointed, shallowly two-lobed, the lower lobe very small, tightly rolled or folded to the upper; underleaves completely lacking. Antheridia and archegonia at the end of the stem; perianth oval or pear shaped, 5-angled, toward the very small, tubular mouth, the angles or wings bearing teeth or spines. Name from Greek *colos,* mutilated, maimed, and *Lejeunea* (which see) since the underleaves are wholly lacking.

Of nine species of *Cololejeunea* in North America north of Mexico, one occurs in Michigan.

EXPLANATION OF PLATE 20

Figs. 1-2, Porella platyphylloidea X5: lower and upper side of stem; Figs. 3-7, Cololejeunea Biddlecomiae: 3-5, lower side of stem X25, 6, detail X40, 7, leaf X80; Figs. 8-11, Lejeunea cavifolia X25: 8-10, lower side of stem, 11, upper side of stem with perianth.

COLOLEJEUNEA BIDDLECOMIAE (Austin) Evans
Plate 20, Figures 3-7

With the exception of the various species of *Cephaloziella*, which are too minute for identification with a hand-lens, this is the smallest liverwort in Michigan. It is widely distributed in our region, but as the result of its small size it is commonly overlooked, as illustrated by my own experience in suddenly discovering it in a glen near Ann Arbor where I had passed it for ten years or more. Search in this locality revealed that many of the shaded erratic boulders harbored this liverwort. The patches of it are a dusty yellowish-green, and look so much like a lichen that it is very easy for one interested primarily in liverworts to pass them over. In swamps in Oakland and Washtenaw counties, *Cololejeunea* grows on the base of arbor vitae.

Under a lens, the small, pointed leaves covered, except for the lobule, with tiny spines, and the complete lack of underleaves distinguish this liverwort from all others in our range. If possible, it should be studied with a compound microscope, after which the characters just enumerated will be distinguished much more clearly with a hand-lens.

LEJEUNEA Libert

Plants medium sized, pale, yellowish- or dark green, branched irregularly or pinnately; leaves overlapping from the base toward the apex of the stem, shallowly two-lobed, the lower lobe (lobule) very small, folded or rolled against the leaf; underleaves present, conspicuous, deeply notched, reaching half the size of the leaf in some species. Antheridia on a short side branch; archegonia on the end of a main stem or branch, perianth oval or pear shaped, bearing five wings or keels near the very small, beaked mouth. Name in honor of Dr. Lejeune, a Belgian physician-botanist.

A very large tropical genus, of which ten species reach the United States and one occurs in Michigan.

Lejeunea cavifolia (Ehrh.) Lindb.
Plate 20, Figures 8-11

Although apparently very rare in southern Michigan, this liverwort has been found on shaded sandstone ledges in the park at Grand Ledge. In northern Michigan it occurs more commonly, growing there on the trunk of trees, especially arbor vitae, as well as on cliffs and ledges of limestone. The plants are pale to yellowish-green and might easily be taken for a *Radula*. The plants are smaller and the leaves are of a different shape, however, and under a lens, the deeply notched, nearly circular underleaves clearly distinguish it, since *Radula* has no underleaves whatever. The lobules are very different, also, being small and inconspicuous in *Lejeunea*.

Frullania Raddi

Plants in thin, dark green, reddish-brown, or nearly black mats on the bark of living trees or more rarely on rocks; stems prostrate, somewhat pinnately branched; leaves overlapping from the base toward the tip of the stem, without teeth of any sort, except rarely on those surrounding the archegonia and later the perianth, oval or nearly circular, deeply two-lobed, the lower lobe very small, usually helmet shaped and hollow, folded back tightly against the lower side of the leaf; underleaves universally present, rounded, notched or deeply bilobed. Antheridia and archegonia on short side branches; perianth inversely heart-shaped, somewhat flattened, very obtusely triangular in cross section, much contracted to the small, tubular mouth. Named in honor of Leonardo Frullani, an Italian statesman of more than a century ago.

A very large tropical genus of which 26 species occur in temperate North America, 7 in Michigan and 4 in our region.

PLATE 21 [88]

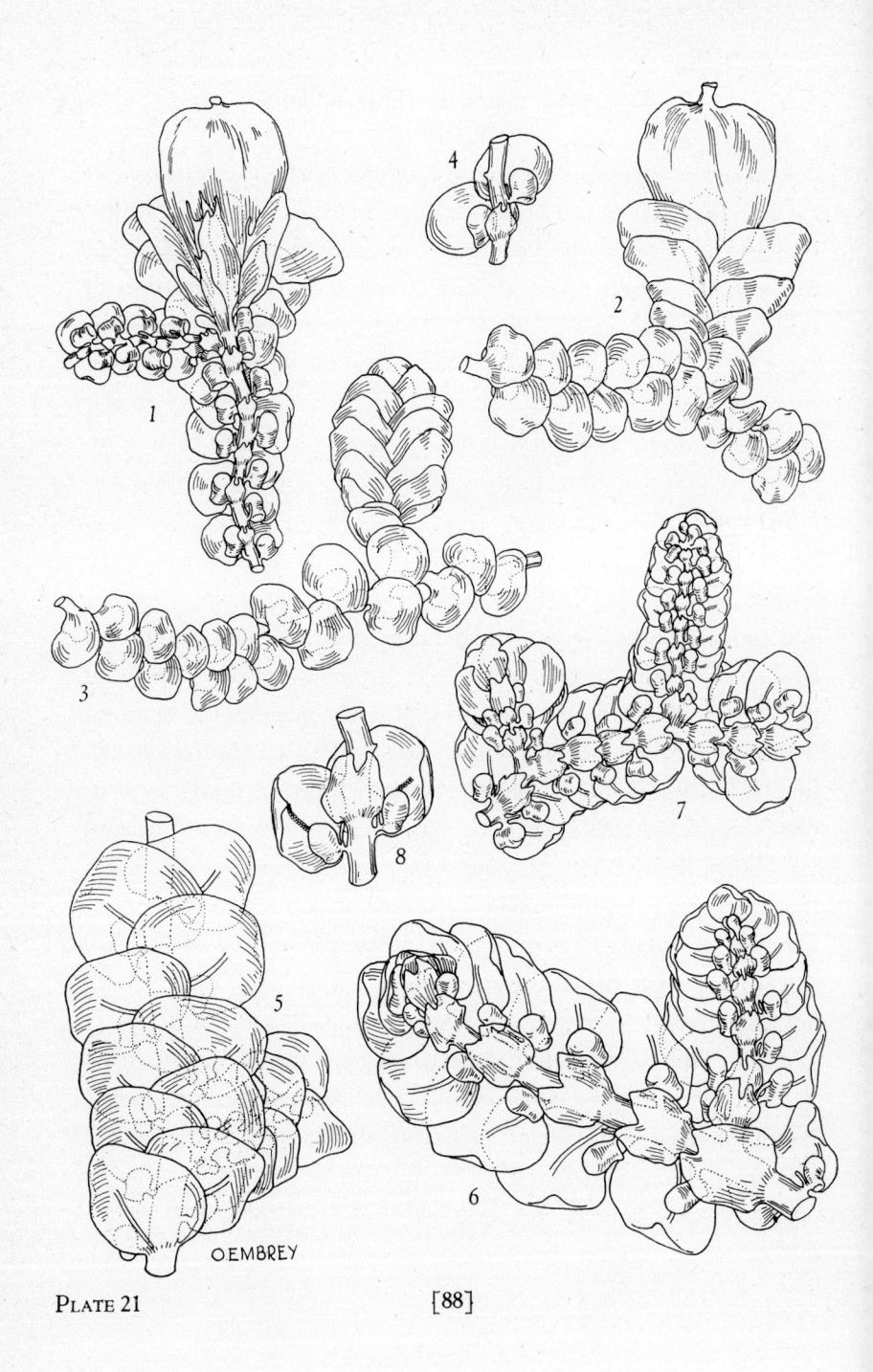

Key to the species of *Frullania*

1. Lower lobe as broad as long; specialized cells lacking from upper lobe; whole plant very dark green or brownish, rarely red (Pl. 21, figs. 1-4)..*Frullania eboracensis*

    Lower lobe much longer than broad; a single or double row of larger, clear reddish cells present in the upper lobe; whole plant with a clear reddish color (Pl. 21, figs. 5-8)...........................*Frullania Asagrayana*

FRULLANIA EBORACENSIS Gottsche
Plate 21, Figures 1-4

This is by far the most common species of *Frullania* in the state, and is to be found on the bark of living trees throughout our area. It becomes almost invisible when dry, but during a rain and as long afterward as the bark remains wet, it forms conspicuous dark green or brown patches. It is especially easy to find on the bark of white birch, and these trees, especially, should be searched for it. The little round leaves on a fine, threadlike stem, the broad, helmet-shaped lower lobes, and the notched underleaves distinguish this genus from any others. The green to black color of this species is very different from the clear brownish-red of the next. Under a lens the two species are clearly distinguished by the broadly rounded lobule of *Frullania eboracensis* and the long, narrow lobule of *Frullania Asagrayana*, as well as the presence of a midrib-like row of clear red cells in the latter species.

FRULLANIA ASAGRAYANA Mont.
Plate 21, Figures 5-8

Like many of the species already discussed, this liverwort is common in northern Michigan, but rare in our area. It grows over the bark of living trees in moist woods or swamps, forming red or reddish-brown patches with a peculiar shining or translucent appearance. It is somewhat

EXPLANATION OF PLATE 21

Figs. 1-4, Frullania eboracensis X25: 1-2, lower and upper sides of stem with perianth, 3, upper side of stem with antheridial branch, 4, detail of lower side of stem; Figs. 5-8, Frullania Asagrayana X25, 5, upper side and 6-8, lower side of stem.

Plate 22 [90]

larger than *Frullania eboracensis,* has much longer and narrower lobules, and larger underleaves, whose edges are bent back. However, the most unique feature appears best only under a microscope: a curious row of larger, colored cells runs through the center of each leaf as a sort of midrib. In some plants will be found leaves which instead of being circular tend to be pointed. Although our two common species of *Frullania* are small and difficult at first to separate with a hand-lens, they are really very distinct and it is possible to learn to recognize them at sight without a lens.

Frullania Brittoniae Evans and *Frullania plana* Sullivant also occur in southern Michigan, but as each species has been collected in our range only once, and as they are exceedingly difficult to learn to recognize without a microscope, they are omitted here.

Anthoceros L.

Thallus dark green, flat, nearly circular, deeply or shallowly divided into lobes, composed, in section, of nearly uniform cells, occasionally with cavities, but never with either specialized air chambers as in *Marchantia* or a thick midrib and a thin wing, as in *Pallavicinia*. Antheridia and archegonia produced in small cavities just under the upper surface of the thallus; sporophyte long-cylindric, green and with stomata above, below with a bulbous absorbing organ (foot) which is buried in the thallus, surrounded at the base by a tubular outgrowth of the thallus (involucre), splitting lengthwise at maturity into two equal parts or valves, thus allowing the spores to escape. Name from Greek *anthos,* flower, and *ceras,* horn, from the hornlike sporophytes. Although 12 species occur in North America north of Mexico, only one is known from southern Michigan.

EXPLANATION OF PLATE 22

Figs. 1-3, Notothylas orbicularis X10: 1, segment of thallus, 2-3, detail of sporophyte and its sheathing involucre; Figs. 4-6, Anthoceros laevis X5: 4, segment of thallus, 5-6, detail of sporophyte and involucre.

Anthoceros laevis L.
Plate 22, Figures 4-6

In moist places throughout Michigan this species is likely to be found, although it has a reputation of being very rare. Near Chelsea and Battle Creek it has been collected on moist clay, on moist, mucky humus at Ann Arbor, and on a dripping cliff of calcareous sandstone at Grand Ledge. The thallus reaches 2 cm. in diameter, and the sporophytes may reach 2.5 or 3 cm. in length. The long, thin sporophytes have a curious grass-like appearance, so much so that this liverwort has probably been passed over commonly as a cluster of grass seedlings. The spores are bright yellow, and are produced in a quantity sufficient to give a yellow color visible to the naked eye to the opening sporophyte. This liverwort is an interesting one and other species should be looked for in our region, especially those with black spores. Under a microscope, it will be seen that each cell of the thallus has only one green body (chloroplast) in it.

Notothylas Sullivant

Thallus yellowish- to clear green, flat, nearly circular, shallowly lobed, much resembling the thallus of *Anthoceros* not only in appearance but also in structure. Antheridia and archegonia produced just under the upper surface of the same thallus; sporophytes produced in large numbers, often paired, oval to short-cylindric, surrounded almost entirely by a tubular sheath, the involucre, from the thallus; the foot large and buried in the thallus, the capsule only slightly green and without stomata, marked with two rows of thick-walled cells, along which the capsule splits when mature, thereby shedding the spores. Name from Greek *noton,* back, and *thylas,* sack, from the sack-like sheaths or involucres surrounding the sporophytes, on the dorsal side of the thallus. Two species of *Notothylas* are known from North America north of Mexico, but only one of them is known in Michigan.

NOTOTHYLAS ORBICULARIS (Schwein.) Sullivant
Plate 22, Figures 1-3

This is one of the most unique liverworts in our region. It has been found by the thousand in several places near Battle Creek by Mr. H. R. Becker of Climax, and will probably turn up elsewhere in our region, after a careful search. The thallus is small, circular, rarely reaching 1 cm. in diameter, and the capsule reaches a length of only about 1 mm. Mr. Becker, who is noted for his discoveries of rare and unusual plants, found most of his specimens of *Notothylas* on the sides of old footprints made by cattle in wet clay. The liverwort seems to prefer clay which remains moist through the summer, as the sporophytes appear in late summer and early autumn.

Glossary

Antheridium (pl. *antheridia*), the spherical or elliptical male reproductive organ of liverworts, which produces the free-swimming sperms or antherozoids.

Archegonium (pl. *archegonia*), the flask-shaped female reproductive organ which produces one egg in its swollen base, and in which develops the sporophyte.

Bipinnate, see *pinnate*.

Calyptra, the greatly swollen archegonium resulting from the growth of the fertilized egg into the sporophyte.

Capsule, the spore-bearing structure or spore case.

Decurrent, (of a leaf) running down the stem as a wing, below the attachment.

Dichotomous, (of a stem) forking equally into two branches.

Dorsal, pertaining to the upper side or back.

Elater, a thread-like structure produced among the spores, usually ornamented with internal spiral bands, which is very sensitive to moisture and helps to disseminate the spores.

Entire, (of leaf margin or perianth mouth) smooth, without teeth of any kind.

Flagellum (pl. *flagella*), (of stem) a branch much smaller than normal, with leaves either strongly reduced or completely lacking.

Foot, the absorbing structure of the sporophyte which is buried in the gametophyte and which obtains food and water for it.

Gametophyte, the green liverwort plant, either leafy or thallose, which arises from the germination of a spore and has for its function the production of eggs and sperms.

Gemma (pl. *gemmae*), a special bud or outgrowth of the gametophyte, which is able to produce a new green plant directly.

Incubous, the type of leaf arrangement in which the leaves overlap, like shingles, from the base of the stem toward the tip. (see *succubous*).

Lobule, a usually smaller leaf lobe which is bent or folded in under the larger upper lobe.

Palmate, (of leaf and stem) a type of branching in which several parts are attached to the same point, resembling the toes of a bird.

Perianth, the tubular, flattened, or angled sheath which surrounds the archegonia and later the calyptra containing the young sporophyte.

Perigynium (pl. *perigynia*), a hollow, underground branch in which archegonia and later sporophytes are produced.

Pinnate, (of a stem) a very regular arrangement of branches along a main stem, resembling the structure of a feather. If the branches are further pinnately branched, themselves, the whole stem or plant is bi-pinnately branched.

Receptacle, (in Marchantiaceae) a region in which the archegonia and antheridia are localized. The archegonial receptacles are usually on stalks, whereas the antheridial receptacles are usually without stalks.

Rhizoid, a hair-like rootlet, by which liverworts obtain water and minerals from the soil, and anchor themselves to it.

Rhombic, having equal adjacent sides with oblique angles between them.

Seta, the stalk upon which the capsule is raised at maturity.

Simple, (of a leaf) not lobed or divided; (of an air chamber pore) surrounded by only one layer of cells.

Spore, a small, usually one-celled structure which is produced in the capsule of the sporophyte, yet germinates into a green gametophyte plant.

Sporophyte, the spore producing part of the liverwort, arising from a fertilized egg and consisting of a foot, seta and capsule.

Stoma (pl. *stomata*), (in *Anthoceros*) a pore bounded by two modified cells, the guard cells, through which gases may enter or leave the sporophyte.

Substratum, the material upon which the plant grows, whether it be bark, soil, humus, rock, etc.

Succubous, the type of leaf arrangement in which the leaves overlap, like shingles, from the tip of the stem toward the base. (see *incubous*).

Thallus (pl. *thalli*), a plant body without stems or leaves, consisting only of a flat, ribbon-like or heart-shaped mass of tissue.

Truncate, (of leaf or perianth) cut off squarely and sharply at the apex.

Underleaf, a usually much smaller leaf on the under side of the stem, next the substratum.

Unistratose, (of a thallus) of one layer of cells only, in thickness.

Valve, one of the four parts into which the capsule of most liverworts separates when its spores are shed.

Ventral, pertaining to the lower side.

Index

Figures in BOLD FACE indicate page on which illustrations occur.

Anthoceros, 91
  laevis, 21, **90**, 92

Asterella tenella, 28

Barbilophozia, 71
  barbata, 20, **70**, 72

Bazzania, 47
  trilobata, 19, **46**, 49

Blepharostoma, 44
  trichophyllum, 18, 45, **46**

Calypogeia, 19, 20, 49, 51
  fissa, **48**, 53
  Neesiana, **50**, 51, 53
  Trichomanis, **50**, 51

Cephalozia, 20, 63, 64, 68
  connivens, **62**, 64, 65
  curvifolia, 67
  fluitans, 68
  Loitlesbergeri, 65, **66**
  media, **62**, 64, 65
  pleniceps, 64, 65, **66**

Cephaloziella, 20, 61, 86
  Hampeana, **52**, 63

Chiloscyphus, 19, 20, 55
  fragilis, **56**, 58
  pallescens, 57, 58, 59, **60**
  rivularis, **56**, 57, 58, 68

Cladopodiella, 67, 68
  fluitans, 19, 20, **66**, 68

Cololejeunea, 85
  Biddlecomiae, 21, **84**, 86

Conocephalum, 28, 29, 33, 34
  conicum, 17, **25**, **26**, 29

Fossombronia, 40, 41
  cristula, 19, **38**, 41

Frullania, 21, 87, 89, 91
  Asagrayana, **88**, 89
  eboracensis, **88**, 89, 91

Geocalyx, 54, 55
  graveolens, 19, **52**, 54

Harpanthus, 53, 54
  scutatus, 19, **52**, 54

Jamesoniella, 69, 73
  autumnalis, 21, 69, **70**, 71

Jungermannia, 72, 73, 75, 77
  lanceolata, 21, 73, **74**, 75
  pumila, 21, 73, **74**, 77

Lejeunea, 86
  cavifolia, 21, **84**, 87

Lepidozia, 45, 72
  reptans, 19, 47, **48**

Lophocolea, 19, 54, 55, 57, 58
  heterophylla, 57, 59, **60**
  minor, 59, **60**

Lophozia, 72
  barbata, 72

Lunularia, 29, 30
  cruciata, 17, 30, **31**

Marchantia, 30, 33, 34, 91
  polymorpha, 17, **25**, **26**, **31**, 33, 35

INDEX

Mylia, 77
   anomala, 20, **76**, 77

Nardia hyalina, 75

Notothylas, 92, 93
   orbicularis, 21, **90**, 93

Nowellia, 65
   curvifolia, 20, **62**, 67

Odontoschisma, 68, 73
   denudatum, 20, 69, 71, **78**, 79

Pallavicinia, 37, 41, 91
   Lyellii, 18, **38**, 39

Pellia, 39
   epiphylla, 18, **38**, 40

Plagiochila, 79, 81
   asplenioides, 19, 20, **78**, 80

Plectocolea, 75
   hyalina, 21, 75, **76**

Porella, 83
   platyphylloidea, 21, **84**, 85

Preissia, 34
   quadrata, 18, 35

Ptilidium, 41, 43
   ciliare, 43
   pulcherrimum, 18, **42**, 43

Radula, 81, 87
   complanata, 21, **82**, 83

Reboulia, 27
   hemisphaerica, 17, **25**, **26**, 27, 35

Riccardia, 18, 35, 36, 39
   latifrons, **32**, 37
   multifida, **32**, 37
   pinguis, **32**, 36, 37, 40

Riccia, 22
   fluitans, 17, 22, 23, 24

Ricciocarpus, 23, 27
   natans, **6**, 17, 24, 27

Scapania, 80, 81
   nemorosa, 21, 81, **82**

Trichocolea, 44, 45
   tomentella, 18, **42**, 44

12-1998
#41 green